THE BRITISH MUSEUM CONCISE INTRODUCTION
ANCIENT GREECE

THE BRITISH MUSEUM CONCISE INTRODUCTION
ANCIENT GREECE

JENIFER NEILS

THE BRITISH MUSEUM PRESS

First published in 2008 by The British Museum Press
A division of The British Museum Company Ltd
38 Russell Square, London WC1B 3QQ
www.britishmuseum.org

A catalogue record for this book is available from the British Library

ISBN 978-0-7141-2259-5

Designed and typeset in Minion by Andrew Shoolbred
and Greg Taylor
Map by ML Design
Cover designed by John Hawkins Design
Printed and bound in Hong Kong by Printing Express Ltd

HALF TITLE (TOP) Lotus and palmette ornament detail from an Athenian krater by the Berlin Painter, *c.* 490 BC.

HALF TITLE (BOTTOM) Painted reconstruction of south metope 4 of the Parthenon.

FRONTISPIECE Detail of rider on west frieze slab 2 of the Parthenon, 447–432 BC.

OPPOSITE Roman copy of victorious Greek athlete sculpture by Polykleitos, *c.* 440 BC.

Contents

Acknowledgements

This book has benefited from the expertise of numerous Greek scholars, many of whom are cited in the further reading. For sage advice on specific chapters I thank Eugene Borza (Chapter 9), Jeremy Rutter (Chapter 2) and Jack Kroll (Chapter 4). I am grateful to the staff of the British Museum and British Museum Press, in particular Lesley Fitton, Ian Jenkins, Axelle Russo, Nina Shandloff and Dyfri Williams, for the privilege of writing this book and much guidance along the way. For their generous editorial assistance I am much indebted to Sheila Cunningham, Katherine Stamm and Wendy Zinn, and to the Dean of Arts and Sciences of Case Western Reserve University, Cyrus Taylor, for moral and material support.

Preface

While the sport-obsessed ancient Greeks would have been delighted by the new stadium designed by the Spanish architect Santiago Calatrava which was built in the city of Athena in 2004, they surely would have been confounded that their age-old festival in honour of Zeus held every four years at the hallowed site of Olympia was being celebrated in places as far afield as Beijing. No doubt they would have applauded the *kabuki*-inspired production of Euripides' ancient tragedy *Medea* staged in Tokyo by the Japanese theatre director Yukio Ninagawa, but would have been appalled by the liberties taken in film versions of Homer's classic tale of Troy, the *Iliad*. Those Greek-speakers who sailed the shores of the Mediterranean and Black Sea for two millennia were progressive and adventuresome, and at the same time traditional and superstitious, especially in matters religious. Their enduring quest for knowledge produced the philosophers Plato and Aristotle as well as a sophisticated navigational mechanism that has been dubbed 'the first computer'. In spite of their fragmentary condition, ancient Greek marble temples and sculpture remain unsurpassed, and Alexander's battle tactics are still studied by military strategists. Thus, whether we are aware of it or not, the achievements of a small group of fiercely independent, free-thinking, highly imaginative people residing in autonomous city-states have continued to play a role in our daily lives.

Unlike some surveys of Greek antiquity which restrict their coverage to the political boundaries of modern Greece, this book aims to encompass the entire Greek world from the Bronze Age to the Roman conquest, and so the reader will encounter discussion of lands outside what many consider to be Greece proper. And while most such texts emphasize the originality and uniqueness of Greek culture, this book will attempt a more balanced view, acknowledging the extent to which the ancient Greeks were influenced by the neighbouring civilizations of the ancient Near and Middle East and Egypt. The goal is to elucidate the unique accomplishments of Greek civilization rather than to provide yet another narrative history of ancient Greece. As will be obvious throughout these pages, the renowned collections of the British Museum, which encompass a vast range of Greek cultural artefacts from the lowliest clay loomweight to the Parthenon marbles, have served as an inspiration for what follows. The interested reader can find many more examples of Greek art and architecture illustrated in the books listed in the bibliography, but the best approach of all is to view the works of art and monuments at the museums and sites themselves, some of which are also noted. I have tried to honour the title of this book by being 'concise'; after all, it was an ancient Greek librarian (Kallimachos of Alexandria) who said 'a big book is a big evil'.

NOTE: All dates are BC unless otherwise indicated, and a list of key dates can be found at the end of the book. As usual in books on antiquity, spelling is not entirely consistent. Some names like Sokrates and Herodotos may look unfamiliar at first, but these spellings are closer to the original Greek, which used 'k' where the Latin uses 'c' and 'os' in endings rather than the Latin 'us'. English transliteration is used for other proper names like Athens and Thucydides which have become common usage. Unfamiliar Greek terms are defined in the Glossary.

Rediscovering Ancient Greece

One of the first works of art to strike the eye of the visitor to a major art museum is often an ancient marble statue, usually dramatically positioned in a central location, like the *Nike of Samothrace* at the top of the Daru staircase in the Louvre or the *Doryphoros* in the Minneapolis Institute of Arts. Such pristine white stone sculpture could be said to epitomize Classical antiquity in general and ancient Greece in particular. And if not an antiquity, then a classically inspired statue will play the part, like the *Perseus* of Canova that stands guard on the balcony overlooking the entrance of the Metropolitan Museum in New York, or the bronze (another important ancient medium for sculpture) *Diana* shooting her bow by Saint-Gaudens in the Philadelphia Museum of Art. The architecture of these vast and stately museums is also frequently derived from Greek models. With their Doric or Ionic columns and triangular pediments – in some cases filled with classically inspired sculpture – they intentionally evoke ancient Greek temples. These evocations of the classical past have shaped modern thinking about this remote, foreign civilization in inspiring but often misleading ways.

Let us take one well-known statue, the discus-thrower, known in Greek as the *Diskobolos*, and consider it in greater detail. Called 'one of the most famous images of the ancient world', it represents a male athlete in peak physical form. He is portrayed young and nude as are many male figures in Greek art. At a moment of intense mental concentration, he is crouching with his body in a zigzag shape topped by an arc formed by his arms – a pose whose efficacy for this competitive event has been questioned by modern athletes. In his right hand he clasps the heavy round disc which has reached the end of its pendulum movement and is about to change direction for the throw. His eloquent silhouette is interrupted by the tree trunk supporting the left leg, a later addition necessitated by the medium of marble. The original was cast in bronze and did not need such intrusive supports, and in terms of colour bronze was more realistic, being brass in tone rather than white like the marble copy (which may have been painted in antiquity).

In the male-dominated patriarchal society of ancient Greece youths trained as athletes in order to become fit warriors in service to their city-states, which

1 Discus-thrower (*Diskobolos*). Roman copy of a Greek bronze original attributed to Myron of the early fifth century BC. From Hadrian's Villa in Tivoli, Italy, in 1791. H. 1.7 m. This Roman version of a Greek original represents a young nude male, bending over, right arm flung back, in the act of throwing a discus. He is certainly an athlete either practising in the gymnasium (a term derived from the Greek *gymnos* which means naked) or competing in the pentathlon at one of the ancient games. His youth and beauty, physical development and mental concentration, harmony and balance all signify the Greek ideal, today as in antiquity. Called by the art historian Walter Pater 'all one had ever fancied or seen in old Greece, or on Thames' side, of the unspoiled body of youth', this classic of Greek sculpture, discovered in 1791, in many ways epitomizes the ancient concept of perfection as expressed by the Attic tragedian Sophokles: 'numberless are the world's wonders, but none more wonderful than man'.

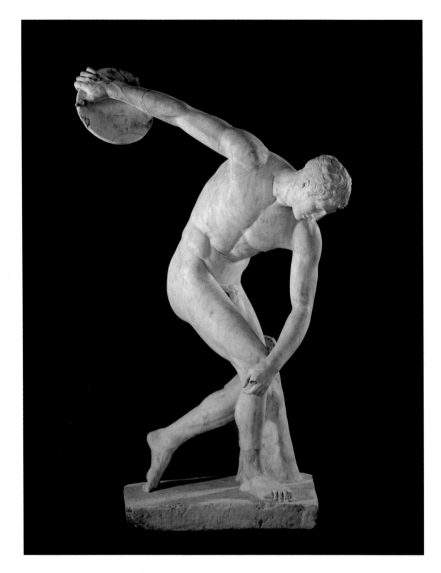

were more often than not at war with one another. Following military service they became statesmen who debated in the assembly and the law courts, attended the theatre and other local festivals, sipped wine and sang poetry at the symposium, and left their wives and slaves to run the household. Many travelled overseas to found Greek emporiums and colonies, and all worshipped their many deities with offerings and animal sacrifices at the ubiquitous shrines and sanctuaries scattered throughout the cities and countryside. Much of what we know of these ancient Greeks, so far removed from us in time and space, comes from old texts, inscriptions on stone, and words scratched on pottery, but also mute works of art, like the *Diskobolos*, and those buildings and objects of daily life that chance to survive.

The *Diskobolos* also exemplifies the route of transmission of much Greek art and culture, namely via the Romans, for this statue is a second-century AD version of a bronze statue of the early fifth century BC. Formerly it graced the country estate of the Roman emperor Hadrian, along with many other marble copies of famous Greek statues. Although the eighteenth-century AD restorer took the liberty of substituting a later fifth-century BC style head with a more naturalistic hairstyle, this and other copies are all that remain to convey the sense of the original by the renowned sculptor Myron. Since the statue is not signed, unlike later works of art, how do we know who created the original statue? As often in studying the Greeks, we rely on Roman writers, in this instance Lucian, who wrote witty mock dialogues in the second century AD, one of which describes this statue in detail and provides the name of its creator.

'When you come in the hall,' he said, 'don't you notice a totally gorgeous statue up there ... ?' 'Surely you don't mean the discus-thrower', said I, 'the one bent over into the throwing position, with his head turned back to the hand that holds the discus, and the opposite knee slightly flexed, like one who will spring up again after the throw?' 'Not that one', he said, 'for the Diskobolos of which you speak is one of the works of Myron.'

Lucian, *Philopseudes* 18

The Roman encyclopaedist Pliny the Elder also mentions Myron and his discus-thrower in a chapter on metals in his *Natural History* of the first century AD, but he misdates the sculptor's career. Thus, without the Romans and their proclivity for Greek art, we would have little inkling of Myron's masterpiece, and the same is true for much of Greek literature, philosophy, science and religion.

Although we cannot rely entirely on our Roman sources, written or artistic, without them we would know considerably less about Greek culture and history. The travel writer Pausanias (*c.* AD 150) was the original Baedeker, composing his extensive *Description of Greece* in Greek for Roman tourists. Educated Romans read and spoke Greek and knew its 400-year-old literature as we know Shakespeare. They not only copied Greek art and architecture, they also worshipped the same gods under Latin names, as in Zeus/Jupiter or Aphrodite/Venus. They carved Greek myths on their marble sarcophagi and frescoed their homes with renditions of famous Hellenistic paintings. Like the Greeks they favoured commemorative statues, although more often likenesses of generals and toga-clad senators than victorious athletes. Their enthusiasm for things Greek was matched only by that of eighteenth-century Western Europeans.

2 Watercolour by W. Chambers of the Townley Collection in the Dining Room at Park Street, Westminster, London, AD 1794–5. H. 39 cm. In this watercolour of Charles Townley's dining room we see a young woman, seated at the base of the statue known as the *Diskobolos*, sketching, while a couple at the back of the room examines another statue. Public viewing and the opportunity to draw ancient statuary served to edify those unable to make the Grand Tour themselves.

Grecian taste

Before its placement in the British Museum, this version of the *Diskobolos* formed the centrepiece of a famous British private collection, that of Charles Townley (1737–1805). Like many cultured gentlemen of the eighteenth century, Townley made the Grand Tour to Italy where famous antiquities were on display in museums like the Uffizi in Florence or the Vatican in Rome; there he would have seen other copies of the *Diskobolos*. Journeying south not once but three times to acquire classical objects, he became an obsessive collector, amassing hundreds of Graeco-Roman marble and terracotta sculptures. Ostensibly such assemblages were intended to improve the taste of the British, and they did in fact help to usher in the Classical Revival style in the early nineteenth century. The sale of Townley's collection by his heirs to the British Museum upon his death in 1805 formed the basis of the Greek and Roman collection, although today much of it has been relegated to the basement because Greek originals are today much more prized than Roman copies.

Another obsession of eighteenth-century collectors throughout Europe was Greek vases, originally thought to be Etruscan since they were first found in

3 Portrait of William Hamilton by Joshua Reynolds, AD 1776–7. H. 2.55 m. As British envoy to Naples, Hamilton formed two important vase collections, the first of which was sold to the British Museum in 1772. It was published in 1768 in what is often considered one of the most beautiful books of the eighteenth century, here seen open on his lap. His prize red-figure vase sits on the floor to the right, and Mt Vesuvius can be seen smoking in the background. His second collection of vases was lost at sea in 1798 when the HMS *Colossus* sank off the Scilly Isles, but it was partially recovered almost 200 years later by a team of professional divers and has now been republished using the earlier drawings as guides to the position of the fragments.

4 Athenian red-figured water-jar (hydria) signed by Meidias as potter, *c.* 420–400 BC. H. 57.5 cm. The pride of Hamilton's collection, this vase signed by the late fifth-century BC Athenian potter Meidias appears conspicuously in his portrait. It is an ordinary hydria or water-jar with two handles for lifting and one at the back for pouring, but is lavishly decorated with scenes from Greek mythology.

ancient tombs in Tuscany. 'Vasemania' describes the passion for Grecian urns which has continued unabated to the present day. An important early sale to the British Museum, for example, was the vase collection of a contemporary of Townley, William Hamilton (1730–1803). The British envoy to Naples from 1764 to 1800, Hamilton witnessed the early excavations of Pompeii and Herculaneum, the Roman cities buried by the eruption of Vesuvius in AD 79, as well as the opening of tombs in southern Italy filled with painted pottery. It was eventually noted that these black- and red-figured vases bore inscriptions in Greek, and in his first edition of *The History of Ancient Art* (1764), the influential German scholar J. J. Winckelmann gave his sanction to their Greek origins.

Greek vases, and especially those produced in Athens, tell us a great deal about aspects of mythology, religion, drama and daily life (the symposium, warfare, athletics, weddings, women and children), evidence for which is often not otherwise preserved. The two narratives on the Meidias vase illustrate how far removed our modern ideals are from those of the Greeks. On the upper register we see two sons of Zeus, Castor and Pollux, with their chariots in the act of abducting women while the goddess of love, Aphrodite, lounges calmly at her altar below. In the lower zone the hero Herakles (Latin Hercules) sits among the lovely ladies known as Hesperides ('daughters of the evening') who are picking the apples of immortality for him, his fearsome club idling at his side. Neither activity is one we might today consider particularly heroic, and yet these three heroes were major Greek role models whose famous exploits were sung by the poets and who were worshipped at shrines dedicated to them. It seems that in the days of the protracted Peloponnesian Wars between Athens and Sparta, at the end of the fifth century BC when this vase was produced, the painters of Athens and their clients were more interested in romance and escapist idylls than in daring deeds. Or as the great connoisseur of Athenian vases John Beazley later described the style of the Meidias Painter: 'Here also there is beauty, the gleam of gold, loves and ladies with soft raiment, and all that is shining, easeful and luxurious: perfume, honey and roses, till the heart longs for what is fresh, pungent and hard.'

In addition to these eighteenth-century obsessions with Greek sculpture and ceramics, there was considerable interest in architecture, in England largely promoted by a fashionable London men's drinking club known as the Society of the Dilettanti. Consisting of British aristocrats who had made the Grand Tour, it fostered expeditions to classical lands to record antiquities. Perhaps the most influential of these sponsored excursions was that of James Stuart and Nicholas Revett to Athens in 1751–3. They made the first 'measured and delineated' drawings of classical buildings, such as the Parthenon and Erechtheion on the Acropolis, which were then published in three elegant volumes as *The*

5 Engraving of the south-west corner of the Parthenon from James Stuart and Nicholas Revett, *The Antiquities of Athens*, vol. II, 1787, ch. 1, pl. 6. Although the Parthenon was first drawn by an Italian traveller and antiquarian Cyriac of Ancona in the mid-fifteenth century, his drawings were never published. It was the accurate and detailed renderings of Stuart and Revett which allowed architects for the first time to become familiar with and reproduce details from the Classical monuments of Athens. Their published drawings inspired buildings as diverse as museums and pigeon coops.

6 Façade of the British Museum designed by Robert Smirke, 1823. With its stately Ionic columns and triangular pediment filled with classically draped allegorical figures, the entrance to the British Museum deliberately echoes Greek temple architecture. In the nineteenth century the building also housed the Royal Library and a collection of natural history specimens, a virtual cabinet of curiosities.

Antiquities of Athens (1762–94). These publications in part contributed to the fashion rage known as 'gusto greco' that overtook England and Europe in the early nineteenth century and which is exemplified by the classicizing façade of the British Museum. This new taste for the classical orders of Greece, as opposed to Rome, was to dominate European and American architecture for decades to come, and continues to be reprised in post-modern architecture.

Although Stuart and Revett's engravings are well known, it is not generally acknowledged that they undertook excavation in order to obtain accurate measurements and consulted classical texts to glean information about the history and function of these ancient buildings. In this sense one could call them pioneer archaeologists, and their interpretations of many aspects of these structures and their decoration are still valid today. However, even they let themselves be misled by Roman authors, in particular Vitruvius, and sometimes altered the evidence on the ground to fit the textual source.

Classical archaeology

This problem also plagued the man who is considered the 'father' of modern archaeology, Heinrich Schliemann (1822–1890). A prosperous German businessman supposedly brought up on the classics, Schliemann firmly believed in

7 Marble portrait bust of Homer, Roman, first–second century AD, from Baiae, Italy. H. 57 cm. Also from Townley's collection, this version of Homer's likeness is probably the one mentioned by Pliny as commissioned by the famous library of the Hellenistic city of Pergamon. Because Homer lived in the eighth century BC before realistic portraiture was the norm, a portrait had to be invented in later times. As the composer of the two greatest Greek epics *Iliad* and *Odyssey*, Homer was an essential component of Greek and later Roman libraries.

the historical basis of Homer's epic poems, such that they could be recovered with the spade. He tested his beliefs first at Troy in north-western Turkey and then at Mycenae in southern Greece, legendary domains of Kings Priam and Agamemnon respectively. In both excavations he found deep deposits of lavish gold body ornaments, jewellery and weapons, which he dated to the time of the Trojan War as calculated by ancient authors, *c.* 1180 BC. But in both instances he was eventually proved wrong. What he had, in fact, discovered were civilizations which had flourished in the earlier Bronze Age and are completely undocumented in our written sources. We now know that the rich inhabitants of the Shaft Graves at Mycenae, which Schliemann located by reading his copy of Pausanias, were the Greek ancestors of those Mycenaeans who may eventually have encountered the Trojans in the twelfth century BC.

Schliemann also wanted to pursue the myth of King Minos and the monstrous Minotaur slain by the Athenian hero Theseus on the island of Crete. He visited in 1886, but did not succeed in buying land for excavation, nor did anyone while Crete was still under Ottoman rule. Tantalizing objects, like a large clay storage jar sent to the British Museum in 1884, had been found on a hill inland from the Cretan port of Herakleion on the north coast by a Greek aptly named Minos Kalokairinos. It fell to the keeper of the Ashmolean Museum at Oxford, Arthur Evans, to begin scientific excavations there in 1900. Because there was little later habitation on the hill and the walls lay close to the surface, Evans' team was able to uncover the labyrinthine 'Palace of Minos' relatively quickly, and he had a better eye for stratigraphy than Schliemann. He also restored the building so that the visitor has a good sense of the multiple floors, grand stairways and open courtyards of this complex structure covering three acres, although today these reconstructions are considered somewhat controversial. As important as the magnificent finds from Knossos were, especially the wall frescoes, Evans' real contribution was his formulation of a new, as yet undreamed of culture, which he termed Minoan. Today every Greek history text or art history volume devotes a chapter to the Greek Bronze Age, the seafaring Minoans and the warlike Mycenaeans, but these predecessors of the Greeks were unknown until a little over a century ago.

What remained for the Bronze Age archaeologists who followed in the footsteps

The Father of Archaeology

This watercolour of 1877 depicts Heinrich Schliemann showing visitors some of the later remains at the site of Troy. At the time many scholars were sceptical that this small mound in north-western Turkey could have been the site of Priam's lofty citadel. It is popular today to denounce the ambitious and self-promoting Schliemann by crediting the English diplomat living in the Troad, Frank Calvert, with the discovery of the site of Troy at Hisarlik. Scholars point to the outright lies in his text (such as claiming that his Greek wife Sophia helped him dig 'Priam's Treasure' when she was in fact in Athens at the time), and charge him with the looting of the Trojan gold, half of which by contract belonged to the Ottoman state. While these charges are probably accurate, it must be emphasized that Schliemann was the person who had the means and the drive to persist in his quest for the Homeric heroes in the face of what many claimed were mere myths. While most scholars of his time were concerned with the historic Greeks, he laid the groundwork for the prehistory of Greece, now a flourishing field within classical archaeology.

8 Watercolour of Schliemann at Troy by William Simpson, 1877.

of Schliemann and Evans was to work out a chronology, to relate the nine layers at Troy to the three distinct levels at Mycenae, and to correlate these with the palatial phases of Minoan Crete. A perceptive observer will notice the tyranny of tripartite divisions – early, middle and late – which derive from the Old, Middle and New Kingdoms of ancient Egypt. In fact it is the absolute dates from the Egyptian king lists that have enabled us to date the prehistoric civilizations of Greece. The Minoans and later the Mycenaeans pursued an extensive trade with the coastal towns of the Levant as well as with Egypt and, happily for archaeologists, scarabs or other objects with royal cartouches are often found in Greek contexts, thus indicating a probable date. In historic times, datable coins provide a similar service.

Fortunately we are on firmer ground when it comes to the historic period of Greece, from which written records survive in the form of texts compiled by contemporaries as well as inscriptions on stone. The two most authoritative

9 Theseus and the Minotaur. Detail of an Athenian red-figured stamnos by the Kleophrades Painter, *c.* 480 BC. H. 31 cm. The Athenian hero Theseus is about to deliver the *coup de grâce* to the already bloody hybrid known as the Minotauros, or 'bull of Minos', thereby rescuing the fourteen boys and girls sent from Athens as fodder for the monster. He uses a sword in an appropriately civilized fashion while his primitive opponent wields a rock as a weapon.

authors are Herodotos, who composed a history of the 'war between Greeks and non-Greeks', that is the Persian Wars (499–479 BC), and Thucydides who wrote about the enmity and ensuing battles between Athens and Sparta, known as the Peloponnesian Wars (431–404). Our word 'history' in fact derives from Herodotos' word for inquiry, *historie.* His unquenchable curiosity led to numerous digressions about the geography and customs of foreign peoples such as the Egyptians and Scythians. He is aptly called 'the father of history' because he was the first to examine the origins and meaning of events rather than simply recording them. The Athenian Thucydides took up where Herodotos left off, and because he was a general in the wars with Sparta, his account, punctuated with speeches, has the credibility of an eye-witness account. Like those of many other ancient authors, Thucydides' text is incomplete (he died before completing it) and so the historic record must always be amplified by the material record provided by archaeology.

10 Large pithos or clay storage jar from trial excavations at Knossos in AD 1878, Minoan, *c.* 1450–1400 BC. H. 1.13 m. It was impressive objects like this metre-tall storage jar that led European and American archaeologists to Crete to uncover the civilization associated with King Minos. Originally used for agricultural produce such as olive oil, wine or grain, it was discovered in the vast storerooms of the palace, which testify to this site being the major civic and religious centre of Bronze Age Crete.

Classical scholarship has established chronological periods for Greek history and culture whose names and dates derive from a variety of sources. The Bronze Age (3500–1100 BC), for instance, takes its name from the prevailing tool technology, whereas the Geometric period (900–700) is named for the predominant style of vase decoration. The seventh century (700–600) is often called the Orientalizing period because many motifs, materials and types of objects came to Greece from the eastern Mediterranean. The Archaic period (600–480) derives its name from the Greek word for old (*archaios*) and its terminal date from the sack of Athens by the Persians. The term Classical is based on the Latin word 'classis', which referred to military groups, but has come to mean 'of the first class' or highest rank, and its dates (480–323) are based on political events. The year 323 marks the death of Alexander the Great and ushers in the Hellenistic period, which ends with the transfer of power in the eastern Mediterranean from Antony and Kleopatra to Octavian, the future Augustus following the Battle of Actium in 31 BC. And the era we know least about because of its material impoverishment (1100–900; see Chapter 3) is appropriately known as the 'Dark Age', although recently in light of important new excavations some scholars have preferred the term Iron Age.

Archaeology today

In the absence of historically recorded destruction dates, classical archaeologists use a variety of dating methods, one of the most important of which is ceramics which are ubiquitous. Earthenware pots were fabricated everywhere in the Greek world and in all periods from the Neolithic to Roman times. Because ancient vases are made of baked clay which is practically indestructible and have distinctive shapes and decoration which change over time (not unlike modern automobiles) and by region, pot sherds found in stratigraphic sequences and especially destruction levels serve to establish a relative chronology with the

11 Marble charioteer, *c.* 460 BC. H. 1.81 m. Excavated in 1979 at the Phoenician site of Motya off the west coast of Sicily, this remarkable statue with its clinging 'wet' drapery demonstrates how advanced the western Greeks were in the techniques of sculpture.

oldest at the bottom and the most recent in the upper levels. When these ceramics styles are correlated to known historic dates, like the Persian destruction of the Acropolis in 480 BC, an absolute chronology is established. The system has been further refined for Athenian black- and red-figure pottery by the pioneering work of the scholar John Beazley. Using connoisseurship methods previously applied to Renaissance painting, he attributed tens of thousands of unsigned vases to painters and workshops in a chronologically convincing sequence which now forms the basis for dating most Classical deposits. Because it was widely exported, Attic pottery is one of the most useful and reliable dating tools used today on ancient sites throughout the Mediterranean.

Today's archaeologists also have the benefit of numerous scientific techniques for dating, ranging from dendrochronology (tree-ring dating) to radioactive carbon, known as Carbon 14 dating. Far more evidence for ancient life can now be gleaned from the dirt of scientifically excavated sites than was the case in the past. Palaeoethnobotanists can identify foodstuffs and seeds retrieved by a water flotation technique, and palynology (pollen analysis) tells us what flora grew in the area in ancient times. The local fauna can be determined by palaeozoologists studying bones, and now DNA analysis reveals the genetic make-up of ancient peoples. Underwater archaeology is a thriving discipline, allowing for the recovery of ancient shipwrecks that provide valuable evidence for trade and seafaring. Survey archaeology serves to locate and plot rather than excavate sites and so expands our knowledge of entire regions in ancient times. And the computer has revolutionized how archaeological data is recorded, synthesized and disseminated.

Established in 1836, the Greek Archaeological Service oversees all archaeological activity in Greece, including the excavations for the modern Athens subway system which alone produced over 30,000 artefacts. Any official excavation or survey project conducted by foreigners in Greece takes place under the auspices of the foreign schools which have been working in Greek lands for well over a century. Founded first, the French School (1846) excavates at the important sanctuaries of Apollo at Delphi and on the Cycladic island of Delos, while the German Archaeological Institute (founded 1874) conducts excavations at the sanctuary of Zeus at Olympia, home of the ancient Olympics, in southern Greece and in the Kerameikos cemetery in Athens. The Athenian Agora (market place) and ancient Corinth are projects of the American School (1881), while the British School (1886) has focused its attention since the days of Evans on Knossos and conducts excavations as well at Sparta, legendary home of King Menelaus and his beautiful wayward wife Helen. Because many Greek city-states established overseas colonies, there are numerous classical sites in Sicily, South Italy, North Africa, Turkey and the Black Sea region, not to

12 Aerial view of ancient Morgantina, Sicily. Excavated by teams of American archaeologists since the 1950s, this remote town in central Sicily exhibits many of the distinctive features of Greek cities throughout the Mediterranean: a central agora surrounded by stoas, a theatre, terrace housing on the slopes, and a grid plan.

mention the many cities founded by Alexander the Great in his momentous march to the banks of the Indus River. As opposed to the rampant looting that still sadly plagues many of these areas, properly conducted excavations utilizing the latest scientific techniques yield priceless information about the ancient Greek world.

One attraction of classical archaeology, for professional and layperson alike, is the thrill of new discoveries, which can be as dramatic as the accidental discovery in 1972 of two life-size bronze warriors by a scuba diver in shallow waters off the coast of Riace in southern Italy or as seemingly simple as some baked clay tablets with strange markings (Linear B script) found in recent excavations at Thebes in central Greece. Even older finds like the Parthenon sculptures or the Antikythera mechanism (see Chapter 9) continue to elicit intense study by scholars who often produce new ways of understanding such intriguing artefacts of the Greek past. In the field of philology new texts are emerging, often from the wrappings of Egyptian mummies which have lain in museums for generations, on scraps of papyrus used for stuffing. Some of these important scholarly and archaeological discoveries are mentioned in this book, but the reader should be aware that new finds occur on an almost daily basis and some are bound to necessitate revising our opinions and interpretations of life in ancient Greece in the future.

Greece in the Bronze Age

When this mysterious group of objects arrived at the British Museum in 1870, Schliemann had not yet begun his excavations at Mycenae and Evans was still a teenager. Yet the presence of an Egyptian scarab of the pharaoh Amenhotep III, who reigned from 1390 to1352 BC, eventually allowed the museum's Keeper of Greek and Roman Antiquities Charles Newton to date the assemblage to the mid-fourteenth century BC. It represents the typical contents of the tombs of Late Bronze Age inhabitants of the island of Rhodes: some ceramic bowls made in mainland Greece, a schematic terracotta figurine of a bull, a gold ring, jewellery, and weapons of bronze (the prevailing tool technology). After excavations from the early twentieth century in Greece produced great quantities of

similar ceramics and figurines, they were recognized as being products of the Late Bronze Age Mycenaeans. The high-stemmed drinking vessel in particular is a typical wine cup of the period, but its decorative motif, a cuttlefish, derives from earlier Minoan ceramics produced on Crete which represented this sea creature more accurately. It is now assigned by archaeologists to phase IIIA2 of the Late Bronze Age, or approximately 1400–1300 BC, and serves as a kind of 'type fossil' for this period. Altogether this assemblage illustrates several features of Bronze Age society which continued well into later Greek times, namely the high status of the warrior, convivial dining centred around the drinking of wine, and far-flung trading contacts.

Two flourishing cultures originated before that of the mainland Mycenaeans: the Cycladic, found in the central Aegean islands beginning in the Early Bronze Age (c. 3000 BC), and the Minoan of Middle and Late Bronze Age Crete. Because there are no surviving texts from these cultures, or at least none that we can read (the various writing systems of Crete are as yet undeciphered), we must rely entirely on archaeological remains. We will examine them briefly before considering the earliest peoples whom we can call Greeks.

Cyclades

The several hundred islands situated in the Aegean Sea constituting the Cyclades (of which only thirty-four are inhabited today) are actually the peaks of submarine mountain ranges. The southern Cycladic islands (Melos and Thera) are volcanic, and since probably the Upper Palaeolithic or Old Stone Age period (c. 10,000 BC) Melos was an important source of a highly desirable raw material, namely obsidian, or volcanic glass. Obsidian is easily knapped into sharp cutting and scraping tools and so was much valued as a trade item at a time when the prevailing technology relied upon implements made of stone and bone. In fact this early trade in obsidian may represent the earliest evidence so far known for long-distance human exploitation of a natural resource. The western islands of Siphnos and Kythnos supplied lead, silver and copper beginning in the third millennium BC. Fine-grained crystalline white marble is the most prized product of the central Cycladic island of Paros, and its neighbour Naxos produced both marble and emery, an abrasive used to polish marble. Because these raw materials have been found far from their places of origin, we can assume that the Cycladic islanders were seafarers and traders from earliest times. The depiction of large oared ships in their art supports this conclusion.

The archaeological evidence for the lives of these Early Bronze Age islanders indicates that they lived in small settlements, cultivated barley, raised pigs, sheep and goats, fished, and buried their dead in shallow cist or stone-lined graves. Most of our information for their existence comes from these graves, which contained hand-made pottery, marble containers and anthropomorphic

13 Group of Mycenaean finds from chamber tombs excavated in Ialysos on Rhodes in 1868. H. of stemmed cup 21 cm. The Egyptian faience scarab in the centre of this group of objects provides what archaeologists call a terminus post quem, or fixed date after which the objects are to be dated.

14 Four marble vessels made in the Cyclades, Early Cycladic I, *c.* 3200–2800 BC. H. (of vessel on left) 10 cm. These handsome vessels of Greek island marble were laboriously made with stone tools before the advent of metallurgy. It is often said that their pierced lug handles were used for suspension, but perhaps they were necessary to secure lids of some other material such as leather.

15 Cycladic marble figurine of a female with folded arms, *c.* 2600–2400 BC. H. 49 cm. Hundreds of these highly stylized marble figurines of naked women have come to light in the Cyclades. The pose is rigidly canonical with the arms folded across the belly, the right always underneath the left, and the feet pointing downwards. Although they resemble dolls, they were not toys and surely served some as yet unknown religious function in life and in the grave.

figurines. Unfortunately, because of the high esteem for these figurines on the part of the international art market during the 1950s and 1960s, nearly ninety percent were looted and so can provide little or no contextual information about the funerary practices of these early Cycladic peoples.

The elegant high-footed marble jar, known as a *kandila*, is a distinctly Cycladic form whose function is as yet unknown. It has a tall neck, thick-walled body and four perforated vertical lugs, possibly for suspension or to secure a lid – and resembles later unguent jars. The placing of valuable storage jars in the grave may suggest belief in an afterlife in which the needs of the body were still catered for. The marble figurine with folded arms is a typical product of the second phase of the Early Cycladic period. Such figures were produced in large quantities and range in height from a few centimetres to over a metre. The breasts and pubic triangle demonstrate that most are clearly female. The sculptor often carefully incised the fingers and toes, and the facial features (other than the prominent nose) were rendered in paint, now mostly lost but preserved on some examples. These figures were never intended to stand and cannot on their own (as the extended feet and flexed knees demonstrate); they may have been carved specifically to lie on their backs alongside the deceased in the grave. In addition to women, some of whom are shown with swollen abdomens and so presumably pregnant, there are a few figurines of male musicians seated on stools or chairs (providing evidence for Early Bronze Age furniture). These lyre and flute players indicate that music was as important to these third-millennium BC islanders as it was to the later Greeks.

Minoan Crete

The largest of the Aegean islands is Crete, and its geographical position made it an important crossroads between Egypt, the Levant and Europe since at least the Early Bronze Age. It is dominated by high mountains and dotted with caves, which from the second millennium BC served as places of worship in the form of peak sanctuaries and subterranean caverns. Agriculture consisted mainly of grain, fig and olive cultivation and viniculture, and the predominant forms of livestock were sheep, pigs and goats. The flourishing Minoan economy must have been based on international Mediterranean-wide trade, as evidenced by the painted depictions of Minoan youths bearing gifts in Egyptian New Kingdom tombs and the large ship sheds uncovered at the site of Kommos on the southern coast. Although we do not know the Minoan name of this island in the Bronze Age, these Cretan figures are labelled 'Keftiu' by the Egyptians, and Crete is referred to as 'Kaptaru' by the Syrians and 'Kaphtor' in the Bible. Hence the letters K-p/f-t should be part of its original name.

Archaeological investigation of Crete has more or less confirmed Homer's poetic description, composed in the eighth century BC:

There is a land called Crete, in the middle of the wine-dark sea,
beautiful and fertile, surrounded by water; and in it
there are many people, countless, and ninety cities …
and among them is Knossos, the great city, where Minos
was king … and conversed with Zeus.

Odyssey 19.172

To date Knossos is still the most extensive administrative centre yet uncovered by archaeology, while numerous others sites throughout the island (Kommos, Galatas, Gournia, Mallia, Petras, Phaistos, Zakros, Khania) had similar palace-like building complexes but on a smaller scale. One of the great conundrums in Cretan archaeology is the identification of these buildings. Are they palaces as the Victorian-era Evans was conditioned to think, with royal rulers like King Minos seated on gypsum thrones? Are they administrative/ redistributive centres as their clay inventory tablets, vast storerooms and workshops would suggest? Or are they religious meccas with their numerous shrines, divine statuettes in precious materials, so-called lustral basins and subterranean pillar crypts? The answer is probably all three, not unlike the palace complexes of the ancient Near East which may have inspired building on this unprecedented scale *c.* 2000 BC. But what distinguishes Minoan palaces from Near Eastern prototypes is the absence of fortifications – a fact which lends credence to the idea of a king heading up a thalassocracy or naval empire to which cities such as Athens may have rendered tribute, perhaps in the form of nubile slaves. Whether these youths in fact had to perform death-defying bull-leaping acrobatics (which may have survived in the legend of the Minotaur) is still open to speculation, but the evidence of Minoan frescoes and statuettes in terracotta, bronze and ivory at Knossos is certainly suggestive.

That a cultural *koine* (highly uniform culture) existed throughout the island in the second millennium is evident from the common typology of the palatial architecture, the widespread use of Linear A script and clay seals for administration, a fairly standard artistic imagery for human figures, and a shared religion as evidenced by the ubiquity of tripartite shrines, the double axe, ceremonial vessels such as rhyta (ritual sprinkling vessels) and elaborate gold rings with scenes of cult. The on-going excavations at the site of Akrotiri on the nearby volcanic island of Thera have demonstrated that much of this culture was exported overseas before the island's cataclysmic eruption *c.* 1600 BC, and in fact the numerous frescoes found there have considerably enhanced our understanding of Aegean seafaring and religious rituals in particular. The discovery of a bull-leaping fresco in the Nile delta indicates the close trading relationship between Egypt and Crete in the sixteenth century BC, and some scholars have even suggested the possibility of inter-dynastic marriages between

16 Bronze group of a bull and acrobat. Minoan, from Crete, *c.* 1700–1450 BC. H. 11.4 cm. A lithe Minoan youth (his lower legs are missing) is represented somersaulting over the back of this massive galloping bovine. A favoured theme of Minoan art, bull-leaping may not have been humanly possible unless the animals were tamed and trained.

the pharaohs and the ruling families of Knossos. However, the most lasting impact of Minoan civilization was on the Bronze Age inhabitants of mainland Greece, as we shall see below.

There is a great variety of architecture on Minoan Crete, from small ordinary houses to country villas to monumental palatial complexes, but the common materials are mud brick reinforced with timber for the upper storeys, set on stone foundations. The Minoan 'palace' consisted of an open-air court at its centre, usually oriented north–south, surrounded by a maze of rooms of various functions. The most readily identifiable are the long narrow storerooms, as they contained capacious clay vessels known as *pithoi*, averaging 1.2 m (4 ft) in height (see Chapter 1, fig. 10). They once contained what amounted to local taxes in kind, such as wine, olive oil and grain. Ceremonial rooms are usually situated on the west side of the courtyard and some of these consist of enigmatic sunken chambers known as 'lustral basins'. Other features which distinguish Minoan architecture are the so-called stone 'horns of consecration' surmounting the façades, the downward tapering wooden columns, often brightly painted, and pier-and-door partitions which promoted circulation of light and air. The palaces were multi-storeyed, and grand staircases with light wells provided access to the various levels. Evidence for plumbing in the form of stone channels and clay pipes is common, and the principal residential quarter of the palace at Knossos even had a flushing water closet and bathtub. Other areas of these complexes were devoted to the manufacture of luxury goods in gold, ivory, imported hard stones and bronze, as suggested by the presence of imported raw materials such as copper ingots, hippopotamus tusks and a special green-flecked

1 Royal Road
2 Theatrical Area
3 Storage pits
4 West Court
5 Store-rooms
6 Corridor of the
   Procession Fresco
7 Stepped Portico
8 South House
9 South Propylon
10 Throne Room
11 Tripartite Shrine
12 Temple Repositories
13 Grand Staircase
14 Queen's Megaron
15 Hall of the Double Axes
16 North pillared hall/
   banqueting hall?

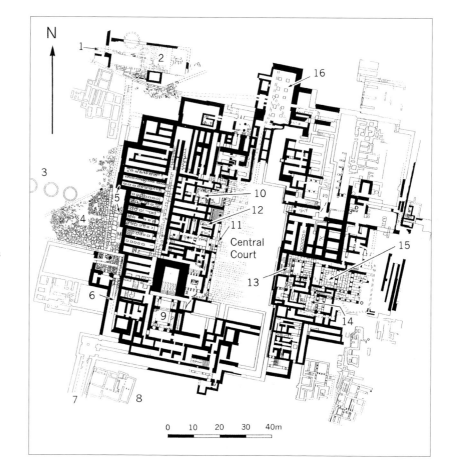

17 Plan of the palatial complex at Knossos. The long narrow rooms at the left are storage magazines, the ceremonial rooms are to the left of the open courtyard, and the residential area approached by a grand staircase is at the lower right. The section at the upper right served primarily as workshops.

porphyry from Sparta. Outside the palaces on the west side there is often a court with a stepped area, possibly for seating or standing during popular assemblies.

The presence of clay tablets at all of these complexes implies their function as administrative centres. Although thus far the language spoken by the Minoans is unknown and the Linear A script remains undeciphered, it is still possible to understand these tablets as inventory lists with numerical indications, as were the later Linear B tablets found in Mycenaean contexts. Another common feature of the Minoan bureaucracy is the use of seal impressions, made by pressing a carved semi-precious stone seal into soft clay which was then used to secure a lid or document, like our sealing wax. Not only do the seal stones themselves survive, with their delicately carved images, but equally important are the sealings; an archive of over 6500 clay impressions excavated in a room of the earlier palace at Phaistos demonstrates the vast scale of the distribution of manufactured and agricultural goods throughout Minoan Crete.

Another distinctive feature of these Minoan palatial structures and surrounding villas, and also of the more modest houses or shrines now uncovered from

18 View of the northern section of the Minoan palatial complex at Knossos as reconstructed by Arthur Evans. A ramp at the lower right leads into the central court and behind the distinctive Minoan columns was a huge painted plaster relief of a charging bull.

19 Theran fresco from Akrotiri, Santorini. A small section of a long 7-m frieze, this fresco provides a glimpse of a Minoan-style island town. Its multi-storeyed buildings face the sea where an oared ship is shown departing. The town is surrounded by a river and in the hinterland a lion chases two deer. With its five towns (one of which may be Akrotiri itself) and extensive flotilla, this unique painting may have served as a sort of portolano, in which case it is by far the earliest extant navigational map.

Ancient or fake?

Acquired by the Boston Museum of Fine Arts in 1914, this delicate statuette, only 16 cm high, is made of ivory and trimmed with gold. With its hands grasping gold snakes, it resembles the Minoan 'snake goddesses' found by Sir Arthur Evans in a palace repository at Knossos. If ancient, it would date to the sixteenth century BC. However, its authenticity has been questioned and recent investigations have suggested that the facial features are too modern in appearance, and the hips are narrower than those of certifiably Minoan representations of women. Scientific testing has proved inconclusive, and the provenance is unknown. Clearly, knowing the find spot of an ancient object not only enhances our understanding of it but also can assure its authenticity. Evans' sensational discoveries on Crete created a market for Minoan antiquities and over a dozen forgeries of such objects are known.

20 Minoan (?) snake goddess statuette, c. 1600–1550 BC or modern.

the volcanic debris on Thera, are fresco paintings on white wall plaster. Figural scenes vary from miniature crowds of people to life-sized processional figures, sometimes rendered in stucco relief. Nature scenes are common with birds, monkeys and cats populating rocky, flower-covered landscapes and dolphins cavorting in the sea. Of particular importance are the Theran scenes of religious rites in which richly dressed girls gather saffron for an enthroned priestess or goddess, and a large regatta sets out from a Minoan-looking town in what might be a new year's festival. Bull-leaping and athletic contests such as boxing are shown, but little hunting or warfare. Given the rarity of extant wall painting in later classical art, this extensive repertoire of lively figurative and nature imagery demonstrates the Minoans' remarkable attempts to capture action and realistically represent their native flora and fauna, especially marine life – also a rarity in the ancient world. That said, they were equally capable of inserting imaginary creatures such as sphinxes and griffins into their otherwise naturalistic landscapes.

21 Minoan agate seal stone, *c.* 1550–1300 BC. Although just over 2 cm wide (here enlarged), this small stone is engraved with a scene of two figures: a man holding a bull by its lead. Such seal stones were probably personal possessions, worn by the owner and used to identify sealed goods in jars and boxes.

If artworks can be trusted as evidence, the ideal physique of the typical Minoan consisted of a lithe body with long legs, narrow waist and broad chest. Men wore a kilt or codpiece and women a flounced skirt with an open bodice revealing their ample breasts; both sexes are adorned with earrings, necklaces and bracelets and have long, curly black hair. Such figures are represented in wall paintings and in terracotta and bronze statuettes, the last often in gestures of prayer. Rarer are the figurines in precious materials, such as the two famous faience snake goddesses from Knossos or the newly discovered chryselephantine youth from Palaikastro in east Crete, who has serpentine hair and rock crystal eyes. The identities of these figures is unknown, but given their composition and high level of craftsmanship they may represent divine rather than human beings.

Much of the imagery on the large gold rings worn by the elite, possibly priests and priestesses, reinforces the idea that the Minoans worshipped a mature female deity and a youthful male god (possibly a forerunner of Zeus who, according to later Greek legend, was born and brought up on Crete). The former is closely associated with nature, either in the form of trees or wild animals, and so may be some kind of fertility goddess. Other elements of the Minoan artistic vocabulary that clearly have religious significance, the exact nature of which is still unclear, are the double axe (or *labrys*, from which our term labyrinth derives), the tripartite shrine and the stylized horns of bulls mentioned earlier. Likewise, the stone ritual vessels known as rhyta that take the form of naturalistic bulls' heads may relate to the bull-leaping performances but were certainly used in religious rites, as most have been found ritually smashed, presumably after their last use.

Although the palatial buildings of the elite and their rich contents are perhaps the best-known aspects of Minoan society, there were also highly developed towns for the lower classes, as the sites of Gournia (excavated by the

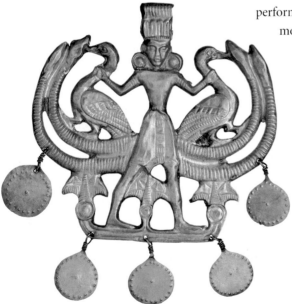

22 Gold pendant from the Aigina Treasure showing a kilted nature deity holding a goose in each hand, probably Middle Minoan *c.* 1750–1500 BC. H. 6 cm. This pendant was said to have been discovered in a tomb on the island of Aigina. Since it represents the finest Minoan goldwork of the period 1700–1500, it was either created in Crete and exported or made on the island of Aigina by travelling Minoan artists.

23 Linear B clay tablets, *c.* 1375 BC. Found by Arthur Evans at Knossos, these tablets record offerings of olive oil to various deities (top) and numbers of sheep at Phaistos (below). On the larger one the shepherd's name appears first in large characters, followed by the name of the district where the flock was kept, the ideograms for rams and ewes, and the number of each. This indicates the wide-ranging administrative control exercised by Knossos over flocks grazing as far as 50 km away.

pioneering female archaeologist Harriet Boyd Hawes in 1901–3) and Palaikastro have demonstrated. At Gournia one encounters a network of narrow cobbled streets, small two-storey houses, workshops of blacksmiths, potters and carpenters, a simple shrine with cult objects and a modest 'governor's mansion', in sharp contrast to the palace-like structures at the major Minoan sites. In fact, such Bronze Age settlements are not unlike the characteristically white-washed small towns that dot the Aegean islands today – their winding streets a deliberate attempt to ameliorate the harsh prevailing winds.

The flourishing culture of Minoan Crete with its extensive Mediterranean-wide trading contacts came to an abrupt and mysterious end *c.*1450 BC. All of the palatial sites were destroyed and abandoned, with the exception of Knossos. Various explanations have been suggested for this sudden collapse: an earthquake (unlikely since the Minoans had immediately recovered from an earthquake of *c.* 1700 BC that had destroyed the first phase of the palaces); *tsunami* from the volcanic eruption of the island of Thera (although this has now been definitively dated to at least a century earlier); or foreign conquest by Mycenaeans from mainland Greece. This last explanation is the most widely accepted, because for the first time warrior burials are found on Crete, and more significantly the inscribed tablets found by Evans in the post-1450 BC levels at Knossos are written in a different script, what he termed Linear B. The only other archive of similar size and with the same script, words and scribal notations is that uncovered in the Mycenaean palace at Pylos in southern Greece, discovered by the American archaeologist Carl Blegen in 1939.

Mycenaean Greece

It was these important excavations at the site of Pylos that helped to answer many of the questions about the Aegean in the later Bronze Age (known as Helladic on the mainland) that had perplexed scholars. First it became apparent that the destructions on Crete were probably caused by invasions of peoples from the mainland who settled at Knossos and adapted the Linear A script to their own language (not the other way around as argued by Evans, who believed the Cretans had conquered the mainland). Second, because the palace at Pylos burned down *c.* 1200 BC, the thousand or so Linear B tablets in the archives were burned and so survived, allowing the Second World War British cryptographer Michael Ventris to decipher this script in 1952. He determined that it was an older form of the Greek language, with words like *elaiwon*, essentially the same root word (*elaio-*) used for olive oil in Greece today. Thus these mainlanders, whom we call Mycenaeans after their major site, could be definitively identified as Greeks. One might well ask why this was ever an issue, and the reasons are that our texts speak of a Dorian invasion of later date ('sixty years after the fall of Troy', according to Thucydides) that brought speakers of a Dorian dialect to southern Greece, and because Schliemann's excavations at Mycenae revealed a culture that looked at the time profoundly un-Greek.

As mentioned in the previous chapter, the deep graves excavated by Schliemann at Mycenae represent an earlier phase of Mycenaean culture, one we call the Shaft Grave period (*c.* 1600–1450 BC). We know little about this era other than what has survived from its elite burials, and unfortunately the majority of the gravesites have been robbed. Schliemann's six shaft graves at Mycenae contained the skeletons of nine men, eight women and two children. Five of the men were inhumed with extraordinary gold face masks, large quantities of bronze weapons (many of which show signs of wear and tear in battle), ceremonial daggers whose blades are inlaid with miniature scenes of hunting 'painted' in precious metals,

24 Mycenaean gold goblet from the Shaft Grave period, *c.* 1500 BC. H. 7.1 cm. Objects such as this elegant cup were used by the elite during their lifetime for elaborate feasts and then accompanied their owners into the grave. It demonstrates the wealth and sophistication of the early Mycenaeans who adopted many art forms from the Minoans on Crete.

25 Reconstructed façade of the so-called Treasury of Atreus, Mycenae, *c.* 1400–1300 BC. H. 10.5 m. This computer-generated reconstruction shows how the façade of the largest tholos tomb at Mycenae would have looked in antiquity. The application of carved red and green marble accentuates the columns flanking the doorway and the relieving triangle above.

and pieces of carved boars' tusks, which were used to reinforce the helmets worn by Mycenaean warriors. Gold, silver and electrum drinking vessels of various shapes and sizes also accompanied the male dead. The female burials contained significant quantities of gold jewellery, textile ornaments and, indicative of their high status, elaborate headdresses. Even the two young children merited suits of gold foil which covered their little bodies from head to toe. Where this sudden wealth and sophistication came from is an open question, but the use of gold masks and a semi-mummified body in shaft grave V suggest contact with Egypt, and many of the more refined luxury goods show strong Minoan influence, if they were not actual imports as seems probable. That these early Mycenaeans had contact with Anatolia (modern-day Turkey) even before their legendary expedition to Troy is indicated by the presence of a silver stag vessel of Hittite type in the shaft graves. The raw material for the large amber beads so popular with the Mycenaeans came from as far away as the Baltic Sea.

The later and more common mode of elite burial in Mycenaean times seems to have been the built tomb, which often took the form of a monumental stone beehive-shaped structure covered by an earthen mound. Known as *tholos* tombs because of their round shape, these cavernous mausolea exhibit highly developed engineering skills, from the quarrying of gigantic conglomerate blocks (some weighing as much as 120 tons) to the careful laying of courses of masonry to create an immense domed interior space with a diameter as large as 14.5 m. The method of construction employed for these monumental tombs is known as corbelling. It is evident in the façade of the so-called Treasury of Atreus at Mycenae, where above the doorway an empty triangle is created by extending each successive course of masonry slightly beyond the one below, thereby creating a void to relieve the weight over the lintel. The door frame at the end of the long *dromos* or stone-lined passage was decorated with engaged columns of imported coloured stone and the relieving triangle was masked by relief sculpture (like the limestone slab still in place above the famous Lion Gate). These

26 Citadel of Mycenae with Cyclopaean walls of *c.* 1250 BC. This view shows the inside of the famous Lion Gate, of which the lintel block weighs over 20 tons. The massive circuit walls of the citadel ranged in thickness from 5.5–7.5 m and were originally about 12 m high.

tombs served for successive family inhumations and so their wooden doors would have been reopened for each new burial. Because they are so conspicuous in the landscape, nearly all of these tombs have been looted.

The Mycenaeans' architectural skills are also exemplified in their massive fortifications, best seen at Mycenae and Tiryns, although traces of Late Helladic walls are still extant on the Acropolis at Athens and elsewhere. With their evident interest in warfare and battle tactics they developed strategic features such as the projecting bastions which enabled them to hurl weapons down on the unprotected right flank of the approaching enemy, postern gates for undetected sorties, and underground water cisterns reached by corbel-vaulted stairways. These fortifications protected the palaces where the king, referred to as the *wanax* in the Linear B tablets, received his subjects and foreign embassies. Called by archaeologists a *megaron*, which is the Greek word for house, the Mycenaean palace consisted of a large square room with a circular hearth in the centre, framed by four columns supporting an upper storey. The walls of these *megara* (pl.) were colourfully frescoed with scenes of battle, hunting, feasting and processions, and the floors were plastered and decorated with painted patterns. In some cases an emplacement for a throne has been found in the centre of the right-hand wall. Visitors approached these grand reception rooms via a two-columned porch and a vestibule so that the plan exhibits a strong axial design, unlike the more indirect approach found in Minoan structures. Likewise

27 Stirrup-handled storage jar with an octopus from Cyprus, *c.* 1300–1200 BC. H. 46 cm. This vase was made on Crete during the Late Minoan IIIB period when the Mycenaeans ruled the island. Its shape matches that found as an ideogram on Linear B tablets, and other vases like this were found at Pylos along with tablets indicating the contents as a high grade of olive oil used as a base for perfume.

28 Late Helladic IIIA terracotta female figurines, *c.* 1400–1200 BC. H. 5 cm. Known as psi, phi and tau figurines because of their resemblance to these Greek letters, these common and cheap figurines are found throughout the Mycenaean orbit, on the mainland and in the islands, and in a variety of contexts including domestic, funerary and votive. Because of their flat-topped caps, which may be forms of the polos worn by female deities, they have been identified as goddesses. They were probably a sideline of the potter's craft, being simply pinched pieces of clay decorated with slip and then fired.

the auxiliary rooms such as storage areas are arranged more symmetrically around the core *megaron* in a centripetal design, as opposed to the more centrifugal scheme of Minoan architecture.

This design principle can also be found in many Mycenaean art forms, even though they take their initial inspiration from Minoan art. A case in point is the typical storage jar with a stirrup handle, probably used for perfumed oils, which is often decorated with Minoan-inspired subjects like the octopus. Here the creature has been transformed from a naturalistic sea creature floating freely in its marine environment into an architectonically symmetrical goggle-eyed motif deprived of two of its original eight tentacles.

In the realm of religion Mycenaean art also shows a striking resemblance to Minoan, so that it is at times difficult to determine what actually constitutes mainland beliefs and rituals. This is particularly true in the fresco scenes of female priestesses and goddesses and on the gold rings with scenes of rituals involving Minoan-looking women. From the nearly life-size painted stucco female head from Mycenae to the ubiquitous small terracotta figurines of draped women it seems likely that the primary deity was female, and the Linear B tablets refer to a goddess with the title of *Potnia*. Because the later Greeks worshipped Demeter and Persephone as Potniai, the Mycenaean version may also have been a fertility and earth goddess. Although many names on the Linear B tablets bear a resemblance to those of the later Olympian deities, they do not appear in a religious context and so might simply be proper names. The only securely identifiable deities are Athena, Enualios (alternative name for Ares),

29 Oxhide-shaped copper ingot from Enkomi, Cyprus, *c.* 1200 BC. L. 69.8 cm. Unworked copper from the extensive copper mines of Cyprus was shipped all over the ancient Mediterranean in the Bronze Age. It usually took this shape which resembles an animal hide because it facilitated carrying and transport. This ingot weighs approximately 37 kg.

Paiawon (likewise for Apollo) and Poseidon, who seems to have been pre-eminent at Pylos. The names of the gods Diktaian Zeus (named for Mt Dikte on Crete, his supposed birthplace) and Eileithyia (the goddess of childbirth) are found only on tablets from Crete. Evidence for cult activity in mainland Greece consists primarily of small single-room shrines with built-in offering tables on which were placed terra-cotta figures, both male and female, and also probably offerings of food and wine. Animal sacrifice was also practised; a detailed image of a bull lying before an altar with its slit throat gushing blood can be found on a unique painted sarcophagus from Ayia Triadha produced when the Mycenaeans controlled Crete.

One of the newest sources of evidence for the Mycenaean economy comes from underwater archaeology, namely the wrecks of merchant ships plying the seas between Egypt, Cyprus, the Levant, Crete and mainland Greece. A 15-m (50-ft) cargo ship wrecked off the southern coast of Turkey at Uluburun *c.* 1315 (a date determined by dendrochronology of a cedar branch carried on board as dunnage) has produced an astonishing array of goods which illustrate the international nature of trade in the Late Bronze Age Mediterranean. The voyage probably began at a Syro-Palestinian port as demonstrated by the 150 Canaanite jars filled predominantly with terebinth resin, but also olives and glass beads. It then called on Cyprus where it amassed over 10 tons of copper, mostly in the form of ox-hide ingots, before it sank. The presence of nearly a ton of tin accords with the prevailing formula for making the alloy bronze (10:1). The ultimate destination of the ship was certainly the Aegean but whether Crete or the Peloponnese is not clear; however, it seems likely that two Mycenaean warriors were on board because of what appear to be two sets of personal belongings (cups, razors, swords, amber beads and seals as in fig. 13).

Like Minoan Crete in the mid-fifteenth century BC, so the flourishing civilization of the Mycenaeans came to a sudden and violent end *c.* 1200 BC.

All the major Mycenaean centres were destroyed and their contents burned (possibly even Athens, although the city claimed otherwise); because most sites were never fully reoccupied we cannot know if the cause was an invasion of foreigners or local insurrections. The prime candidates for invaders are the so-called Sea Peoples, documented in Egyptian sources as pirates who caused havoc throughout the eastern Mediterranean in the late thirteenth century. Confirmation of this theory can perhaps be found in the tablets from Pylos which indicate that 800 men were being sent to watch the coast, immediately before the palace and its contents were burned to the ground. The evidence for internal strife can be found in epic poetry which tells of discord at home during the long drawn-out Trojan War (for instance, Penelope and her freeloading suitors at Ithaka) and considerable upheaval upon the heroes' return (such as the murder of Agamemnon at Mycenae).

Whatever or whoever decimated the Mycenaeans, their legacy to the later Greeks was never completely erased. In spite of the loss of writing, the end of monumental stone architecture, the cessation of international trade and a serious decline in artistic production of all kinds, much survived to re-emerge in historic times, as we shall see. Although the sophisticated social and economic network and the cultural *koine* established by the Mycenaeans was lost forever, poetry and song must have endured, keeping alive the warrior ethos and the tales of gods and heroes which form the core of later Greek literature, art and religion.

3

The Emergence of Greece

Most surveys of Greek civilization gloss over the centuries intervening between the collapse of the Mycenaeans and the 'reawakening' of Greece *c.* 750 BC. The eighth century has been dubbed the 'Greek Renaissance' and justifiably so, since Homer was then composing his epic poems, iron tools and weapons were replacing bronze, the Olympics were organized (the traditional founding date is 776) and the alphabet was adapted from Phoenician script. Astonishingly, all of these remarkable creations of the Greeks are still with us today. The term 'renaissance' derives from the fact that the preceding three centuries (1100–800) constituted what we have traditionally called the Greek 'Dark Age', on the analogy with medieval Europe. But just as we now view the so-called Dark Age of Europe as an important formative period, so too with the Early Iron Age (as some prefer to call it) in Greece. Excavations such as those conducted at the sites of Kavousi on Crete, Perati in Attika, Zagora on the island of Andros and especially Lefkandi on Euboia have revealed an advanced state of 'Dark Age' culture previously unsuspected. Equally important, these excavations have demonstrated some forms of continuity, a frayed but nonetheless unbroken link with the Bronze Age past in the areas of religion and art.

One of the major questions that has perplexed scholars of ancient Greece is how a new civilization arose following the cataclysmic meltdown and cultural disintegration at the end of the Bronze Age. How encompassing was the break with the past and what aspects of later Greek culture as we know it survive from the Bronze Age? To what extent is historical Greece a consequence of renewed contact with the more advanced civilizations of the Near East and Egypt and to what extent is it indigenous? What was the catalyst for the development of what we call 'the Greek way', namely a culture of independent, self-governing, militaristic city-states? Because the period between the collapse of the Mycenaean society and the rise of Classical Greece (*c.* 1200–700 BC) is without texts and lacks much in the way of material culture, these questions are difficult to answer. Most of the evidence for social and cultural development must be gleaned from modest burials and remote sites. Of the former Mycenaean citadels, only at Athens, which escaped major destruction at the end of the Bronze Age, can a continuous occupation be traced, and it is from cemeteries here that an uninterrupted pottery sequence has been established, which in turn

30 Three belly-handled amphorae from Athens (top to bottom): Sub-Mycenaean, *c.* 1100–1050 BC (H. 19.7 cm); Proto-Geometric, *c.* 950–900 (H. 36 cm); and Middle Geometric, *c.* 850–800 (preserved H. 47 cm). These earthenware jars produced in Athens over a period of 300 years demonstrate the changing shapes and systems of decoration (curvilinear to rectilinear) that help archaeologists establish a chronology for periods in which there are no written records. This particular type of amphora known as the belly-handled was used for the cremated remains of women, while men were buried in amphorae with handles at the neck.

has given names to the chronological phases of this period: Sub-Mycenaean, Proto-Geometric and Early, Middle and Late Geometric. More recent archaeological investigation beyond the major sites, however, is beginning to shed more light on this formative era, and it seems that while there were many innovations, some of which can be attributed to foreign influence, there was also more continuity with the Mycenaean past than previously realized.

Lefkandi

One site which has revolutionized our understanding of the so-called Dark Age is that of Lefkandi, on the western shore of the island of Euboia facing and in close proximity to the region surrounding Athens, known as Attika. Here in 1981, when a Greek landowner began to bulldoze a hill (known as 'Toumba') to construct his summer home, traces of a remarkable building datable by pottery to *c.* 1000 BC came to light. Unprecedented in scale for this period, the stone foundations of this apsidal structure measure nearly 10 by 45 m, and in all probability a colonnaded wooden veranda surrounded it, except at the east entrance. With its east–west orientation, considerable length and wooden colonnade, it bears a remarkable resemblance to some of the earliest Greek temples,

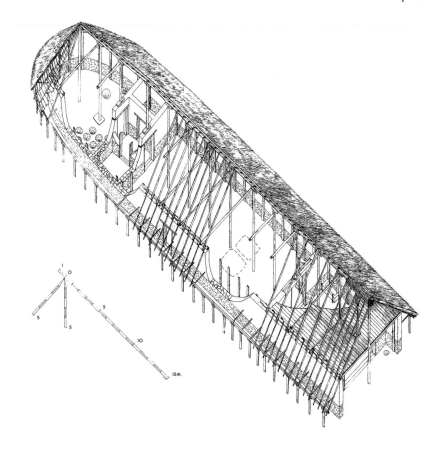

31 Reconstruction of the 'heroon' at Lefkandi, tenth century BC. L. 45 m. This elongated building, originally a ruler's residence and later his tomb monument, is perhaps a prototype for the later Greek temple.

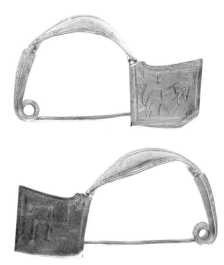

32 Gold earrings and fibulae with incised catch plates, from Athens, eighth century BC. Gold was fairly rare in Geometric tombs, but eighth-century graves in Athens have produced some fine pieces like these fibulae or safety pins, used to fasten garments, and disc earrings. While the pins have incised decoration on the catch plates, the earrings are decorated with minute granulation, forming wave and zigzag patterns. Both display forms of the meander, a characteristic motif of this period.

evidence for which appears only some 300 years later. The first major temple at Olympia constructed around 600 BC was only slightly larger (19 x 50 m). Even more astonishing than the monumental architecture were the lavish burials found within the building, which suggest contact with the eastern Mediterranean as well as a knowledge of 'heroic' burial rites as recorded later in Homeric epic. In the middle of the central room were two large shafts, side by side, one of which contained a double burial: the cremated remains of a man (aged thirty to forty-five) placed in a bronze amphora along with a richly woven cloth and the inhumed body of a woman in her twenties, bedecked in gold. The typical warrior's kit (sword, spear and razor) constituted the male grave goods, while the female's consisted of gold earrings, hair coils, necklace and, most astonishingly in this pre-Madonna era, an item of apparel that resembles a gold bra. In the second grave were the skeletons of four horses, lying where they no doubt fell, their bits still clenched in their teeth. Sometime shortly after these burials the building was demolished and a huge earthen mound erected over the site; a cemetery containing both cremations and inhumations then developed at the eastern end of the mound, as if in homage to the town's most illustrious leader.

More significant than the grave goods themselves, which are extraordinarily rich for such an impoverished period, is the fact that some were foreign imports and heirlooms. The woman's pectoral, for instance, has been shown to be of a type common in Babylon around the year 2000 BC. The bronze vessel containing the cremation, decorated with files of animals, was imported from Cyprus. These objects as well as other imports found in the later adjacent graves demonstrate that the residents of Lefkandi, although primarily herdsmen, had wide-ranging trade contacts in the eastern Mediterranean. Also significant is the elaborate burial rite for the wealthy couple, perhaps the chief of the tenth-century settlement and his wife (possibly a foreign bride, given the different burial treatments). His body was honoured like that of a Homeric hero as described in Book 23 of the *Iliad*, in which Achilles constructs an enormous funeral pyre, sacrifices four horses, and then builds a large mound for his beloved companion-in-arms Patroklos. As a result of these similarities some scholars refer to the 'Toumba' at Lefkandi as a hero shrine, although none of the typical offerings were found in the vicinity. More likely the rich elites of the early Iron Age who rated such elaborate burials were the actual warriors and chieftains about whom Homer and Hesiod sang in their poetry centuries later. The treatment accorded the warrior-chief of Lefkandi, his wife and his house, which was ritually destroyed after his death, indicates that he was granted the *time* or honour so avidly sought by Homeric heroes. The valuable foreign objects indicate his rank and perhaps also the concept of gift exchange among elites, so often described by Homer. One of the silver bowls awarded at Patroklos' funeral games originated in Sidon and was given by Phoenicians to the king of Lemnos whence a Trojan ally used it to ransom the body of one of Priam's slain sons. Thus already in the tenth century BC the rulers of small unfortified hilltop settlements were living the life described in the *Iliad* and the *Odyssey*.

Homer

At the crux of our understanding of the emergence of Greece lies Homer, the supposedly blind bard who composed his epics in the latter half of the eighth century. The most famous and influential poems in antiquity, they focused on the trials and tribulations of two individual Greek heroes, Achilles at Troy and Odysseus on his voyage home to Ithaka. Probably not codified and actually written down until the sixth century BC, these heroic sagas were part of an extensive oral tradition of storytelling in early Greece. Poetry was sung to the accompaniment of the lyre, and the frequent textual repetitions helped the performer remember his lines, while the common epithets like 'swift-footed Achilles' or 'rosy-fingered dawn' arose from their conforming to the special epic meter known as dactylic hexameter. For generations to come these colourful sagas provided fodder for poets, playwrights and artists.

Although its title derives from one of the names for Troy (Ilium), the *Iliad* does not narrate the entire story of the Trojan War from the Judgment of Paris to the famous ruse of the wooden horse. Rather it focuses on Achilles' rage against his supreme commander Agamemnon, as stated in the very first lines of the poem:

Sing, muse, the anger of Peleus' son Achilles and its devastation,
which put pains thousand fold upon the Achaeans [i.e. Greeks],

33 Achilles fighting the Trojan prince Hector. Detail of an Athenian red-figure volute-krater attributed to the Berlin Painter, *c.* 500–480 BC. H. 63.5 cm. In the centre of this frieze-like composition Achilles advances to the right (the lucky side in Greek art) against the greatest Trojan warrior, Hektor. Beyond the duelling heroes are their patron deities: Athena urging on her favourite Achilles, and Apollo abandoning Hektor to his inevitable fate. Athenian vase painters were familiar with the story of the *Iliad* because it was recited in its entirety every four years at the civic and religious festival of the Panathenaia.

hurled in their multitudes to the house of Hades strong souls of heroes,
but gave their bodies to be the delicate feasting of dogs, of all birds,
and the will of Zeus was accomplished since that time when first there stood
in the division of conflict Atreus' son the lord of men [i.e. Agamemnon]
and brilliant Achilles.

The poem begins with the dark imagery of death and burial (or lack thereof) and ends on a similarly lugubrious note with the cremation and laying to rest of the greatest Trojan warrior Hektor (Latin Hector). The duel between Achilles and Hektor represents the climax of the poem, and Achilles' victory gains for him the *kleos* or fame for which he sacrifices his young life. In spite of his often uncontrollable anger, Achilles represents the warrior ideal which in Homeric society meant more than mere prowess in combat: an eloquent speaker, generous host, loyal friend, accomplished musician, dynamic and inspiring leader, and an unsurpassed fighter. The narrative takes place near the end of the ten-year war and the action amounts to a mere four weeks; but during this time Achilles argues with Agamemnon, sulks in his tent, loses his life-long companion Patroklos, conducts on his behalf a lavish funeral complete with athletic and equestrian contests, kills Hektor in single combat and mutilates his body, and eventually allows its ransom by the grief-stricken Priam. He suffers a tumult of emotions from unquenchable ire to abject sorrow, and finally pity for his enemy.

34 Odysseus being rowed past the Sirens. Athenian red-figure stamnos attributed to the Siren Painter, *c*. 475 BC. H. 35.2 cm. One of the most detailed images of this vivid scene from the *Odyssey* (Book 12), this vase painting not only shows the hero of the epic tied to the mast of his ship but also small details like the wax in the ears of his crew. These precautions were necessary because, according to Homer, the Sirens' singing drove sailors mad so that their boats crashed on the shore where they were left to rot.

The *Odyssey*'s narrative is quite different, and some scholars suspect it was composed by a different author. Less of a psychological portrait, it deals with the wily Odysseus, who manages to survive the ten-year-long Trojan War and wander for another ten years around the Mediterranean, losing all his companions in the process, before he eventually arrives home to Ithaka and his long-suffering faithful wife, Penelope. Here he meets the challenge of ridding his home of the parasitic suitors who in his long absence have lived off his household and wooed his wife. He succeeds in re-establishing his sovereignty, triumphing against the odds as always with his ingenuity – and the help of his patron goddess Athena. In contrast to the *Iliad*, which can almost be read as history, the *Odyssey* has many more elements of fantasy, as told in the long flashback tale of the hero's wanderings on the sea. Here he encounters monsters (the one-eyed giant Cyclops, the dog-bodied Skylla), temptresses (Calypso, Sirens) and a witch (Circe), all of whom attempt to prevent his homecoming. With Athena's counsel he manages to outwit them all, as when he stuffs his rowers' ears with wax so he can sail unscathed by the Sirens, tied to the mast of his ship while listening to their irresistible song – irresistible of course because it recounts the *kleos* of heroes.

The wine-dark sea

Leaving aside the more fantastic aspects of Odysseus' story, an audience in eighth-century Greece may well have related to his harrowing adventures of travel by sea. Whirlpools, storms, shipwrecks, landings in hostile territory – all must have been common experiences among the seafaring Greeks, who at this time were undertaking trading excursions to the Levant (as suggested by the imports at Lefkandi and elsewhere) as well as relocating large parts of their population to colonies and emporia overseas both east and west. In Book 4 of the *Odyssey* the hero claims to have sailed far and wide in the Mediterranean: 'Much did I suffer, and wandered much before bringing all this home in my ships when I came back in the eighth year. I wandered to Cyprus and Phoenicia, to the Egyptians, I reached the Ethiopians, Eremboi, Sidonians and Libya.' Because the Phoenicians, who were Canaanites residing in modern-day Lebanon, do not make an appearance before *c.* 1000 BC, Homer is clearly here describing travel in the early first millennium BC (Iron Age) rather than the late second (Bronze Age). Odysseus' narrow escape through the twin perils of Skylla and Charybdis is clearly a reflection of the treacherous waters in the straits of Messenia, where many Greek ships must have come to a sorry end.

35 Late Geometric spouted krater with a multi-oared ship, *c.* 730–720 BC. H. 30.9 cm. Although this scene is often interpreted as mythological, such as Theseus abducting Ariadne from Crete or Paris kidnapping Helen, it could also simply depict a common occurrence in eighth-century Greece, namely a Greek seafarer snatching a foreign bride. The wreath she holds suggests nuptials, and the shield in the hold of the ship indicates his warrior status.

36 Two nude female figurines: Greek double bone figurine, possibly a goddess, from Rhodes, *c.* 700–650 BC (H. 6 cm); and Phoenician terracotta figurine from Sardinia, sixth century BC (H. 17 cm). Female nudity was rare in Greek art before the mid-fifth century BC, when the sculptor Praxiteles produced a statue of the nude Aphrodite. The Greek figurine is modelled on a Near Eastern female goddess like the one at the right – another example of the 'orientalizing' art of the seventh century.

Evidence for seafaring can also be found on painted earthenware vases produced in the early Iron Age, decorated in what we call the Geometric style. The earliest figurative scene in Geometric art (on a Middle Geometric cup found at Eleusis) depicts a sea battle, and oared ships are regularly featured on large Late Geometric kraters, used for mixing water and wine. Already around 1000 BC, Greeks were establishing colonies along the west coast of Turkey, and the earliest colony in the west (Naxos on the east coast of Sicily) is dated by the historian Thucydides to 735. However, before establishing permanent settlements the Greeks came as traders, and in the case of Italy founded an emporium near Naples (Pithekoussai on Ischia) in the mid-eighth century, enabling them to obtain valuable metal ores from the Etruscans to the north.

Through trade and colonization, and also as pirates and mercenaries, the Greeks again came into contact with the more developed civilizations of the Near East and Egypt. Their confrontation with the sophisticated artistic products of these regions had a profound effect on their own nascent art forms. Some of the earliest sculpted images of women, for instance, show them naked in spite of the fact that female nudity was never the norm in Greek culture. Clearly these early figurines, often of imported ivory, were carved in imitation of the Near Eastern fertility deity Astarte, and they may represent the first Greek images of the goddess of sex and love, Aphrodite.

However, the most important innovation the Greeks took from the Near East was the alphabet, which they adapted from the Phoenician script as noted by the historian Herodotos. The Phoenician alphabet consisted of twenty-two consonant signs, some of which the Greeks changed to vowels. We do not know

Alpha, Beta ... Whence the alphabet?

According to the historian Herodotos the Greeks learned to write from the Phoenicians, and he further states that the Greeks called their letters *phoinikeia* or 'Phoenician things'. Both the manner in which the letters are written and their order from *alpha* to *tau* confirm this derivation. As one can see in the transformation from Semitic script to Greek there is a pronounced tendency to make the letter forms more vertical and rectilinear, thus conforming better to the prevailing Geometric-style decoration. The Greeks needed fewer consonants than the Phoenicians and so changed some letters to vowels, which are lacking in Semitic scripts. In addition they invented new signs for double consonants (*phi*, *chi*, *psi*) and added them on at the end.

PHOENICIAN		GREEK		
'ālep	KKK	ΔΔΛ	Λ	alpha
bēt	9 9	ᗺ ᗺ B	B	bēta
gīmel	ᒋ ᒊ	ᒋ ᒊ C	Γ	gamma
dālet	ᐁᐁᐁ	ᐅᐁD	Δ	delta
hē	ヨ ヨ	ᓭᓭE	E	e psilon
wāw	Y Y Y	F F ᒐ		digamma
zayin	I ᕱ I	I ᕱ I	I	zēta
ḥēt	ᗷ ᗷ ᗷ	ᗷ ᗷ H	H	eta
ṭēt	⊗ ⊕	⊗ ⊕ ⊙	Θ	thēta
yōd	Z Z ᔓ	ᔓ ᒐ ᕦ	I	iōta
kap	ᏉᏉ ᧵	K K K	K	kappa
lāmed	ᒪ ᒪ ᒪ	ᒪ ᒋ Λ	Λ	lambda
mēm	ᔓ ᔓ ᕼ	ᒭᒭM	M	mu
nūn	ᔓ ᔓ ᕼ	ᒭ ᒭ N	N	nu
sāmek	ᕚ	ᕚ ᕟ ᕗ	Ξ	ksi
'ayin	O	O	O	o mikron
pē	ᒄ ᒑ	ᒋ ᒋ	Γ	pi
ṣādē	ᕁ ᕼ	M		san
qōp	ᖽ ᖾ φ	Φ ᖽ		qoppa
rēš	ᖟ ᖰ	P D ᖆ	P	rhō
śin/šin	W	ᕗ ᒐ ᕚ	ᕉ	sigma
tāw	+ X	T	T	tau
		ᕉ ᕉV	Y	u psilon
		Φ ⊕ ᖣ	Φ	phi
		X +	X	chi
		ᕉV	Ψ	psi
		ᙯᙯᙯ	Ω	ō mega

Phoenician and Greek alphabets.

37 Late Geometric pitcher with scenes of women mourning at the biers of two dead persons, from Athens, *c.* 720–700 BC. H. 44.3 cm. The rites for the dead are the earliest figurative scenes in Greek painting: they include the laying out of the body (*prothesis*) on its bier and its subsequent transport to the cemetery (*ekphora*). Women are regularly shown as the chief mourners, as here. This vase is unusual in that it includes two corpses, rather than the usual one.

exactly where this momentous step took place – it could have happened in a variety of locales – but it was most likely by the Euboians, who were the earliest and most adventuresome traders. They established a trading colony at Al Mina at the mouth of the Orontes in Syria *c.* 800, and also came into contact with the Phoenicians at their colony of Pithekoussai in the Bay of Naples. Early Greek inscriptions have been found at both sites, and some are written in hexameters which has suggested to scholars that Homeric epic rather than trade was the impetus for the transmission of writing. One of the oldest substantial inscriptions is the three-line verse inscribed on a Late Geometric skyphos of *c.* 730 found in a burial at Pithekoussai: 'I am the cup of Nestor, a joy to drink from. Whoever drinks this cup, straightway the desire of beautiful crowned Aphrodite will seize.' It is a witty joke referring to both the famous gold cup of King Nestor described in the *Iliad* and the effects of strong wine on the drinker.

Geometric art

Much of what we know about life in Iron Age Greece comes from the contents of burials where the elite deposited many of their personal possessions such as bronze or iron weapons and gold jewellery. If they could not take their larger possessions with them, they would occasionally substitute clay models. Examples include the terracotta horses which serve as handles for the lids of large round pyxides (cosmetic boxes), or small-scale beehive-shaped granaries, obvious references to the horse-raising, land-owning aristocracy. Their elaborate funerals are often depicted on Attic Late Geometric vases, on which the most common scene is the *prothesis* or laying out of the body on a bier. As always in Greek funerary ritual, women were the chief mourners and are shown surrounding the deceased, wailing and tearing their hair with upraised arms. These earliest figurative scenes in Greek art were no doubt inspired by the function of the vases themselves, either as cinerary urns or, in the case of larger and even monumental vases, as grave markers in the cemetery. The rendering of the human figure is deliberately 'geom-etricized' in sympathy with the overall recti-linear ornament that prevailed on ceramics of this period.

No life-size sculpture exists from this early period of Greek art, but bronze workers

38 Model of a granary with Geometric patterns, from Athens, *c.* 730–700 BC. H. 9.5 cm. We can only make educated guesses about the function of strange objects like this found in Athenian graves of the eighth century. It could be a small-scale model of a granary and thereby indicate the landed wealth of the grave's occupant. Alternatively, given its resemblance to a beehive, it might be a clay version. Honey could represent purity and incorruptibility and was often served as an offering to the dead.

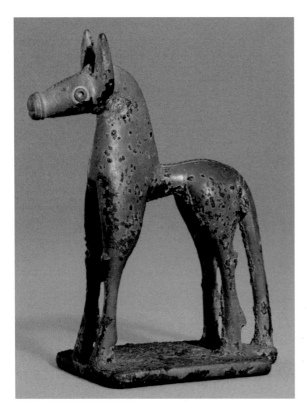

39 Bronze Geometric horse said to be from Arkadia, *c.* 700 BC. H. 10 cm. Probably manufactured in Sparta, this solid-cast bronze horse on its cut-out stand was a common dedication in sanctuaries during the later eighth century. The horses are especially prevalent among the early finds at Olympia, an area of wealthy herdsmen.

were busy producing small, solid-cast statuettes of humans, birds, animals and even beetles. These served as dedications to the gods in sanctuaries throughout Greece, but the site of Olympia in particular has produced an enormous quantity, especially horses. All are stylized in the manner of Geometric vase painting, with thin bodies, triangular haunches and tubular muzzles. The most lavish dedications in these sanctuaries were large bronze tripods, objects well known from epic in which they were often awarded as prizes in athletic contests. At the site of Olympia, where by far the most have been excavated, they may have been dedications to Zeus by victorious athletes, as the Olympic Games were reputedly founded here in the eighth century.

One of the first artistic centres to break away from the tyranny of the restrained Geometric style was the wealthy city of Corinth, ideally located at the isthmus between central Greece and the Peloponnese. Here in the late eighth century vase painters suddenly adopted curvilinear plant forms, foreign beasts such as lions, and human figures drawn in outline rather than the earlier silhouette. This abrupt shift to a new style, in addition to subject matter, was surely inspired by the more naturalistic imagery of Near Eastern art as filtered though the Phoenicians (such as the silver bowl mentioned earlier). Known in art history as 'orientalizing' because of its Eastern origins, this infatuation with foreign motifs caused a virtual artistic revolution as artisans throughout Greece adapted the new style and imagery to their traditional media of pottery and bronze-casting.

Much of the more fantastic (what we would call mythological) imagery of Greek art was also adapted from the East. A case in point is the griffin which like many monsters was a hybrid, in this instance a combination of a lion's body, bird wings and an eagle's beak. The Greek as opposed to Eastern griffin is distinctive with its tall ears and prominent knob on the brow. In seventh-century metalwork griffin heads were used to decorate the rims of large bronze cauldrons, presumably to ward off evildoers in the sanctuaries where they were often dedicated. This particular type of bronze cauldron originated in distant Urartu (Armenia) and was exported throughout the Mediterranean. While the sheet metal bowls have often disintegrated, the cast bronze griffin heads survive

40 Early Proto-Corinthian aryballos, *c.* 690 BC. H. 6.8 cm. While the warrior and his squire are Greek themes, the 'tree of life' in the centre and the lion chasing a deer, beyond the tree at the right, derive from foreign sources. The ornamental motifs filling the background also suggest Eastern influences on the painted decoration of this small perfume flask produced in Corinth, a major ceramics centre in the seventh century.

in great numbers and are handsome examples of the metallurgical skills of Greek craftsmen. Other hybrids imported from the Near East and Egypt include the sphinx, hydra and siren, but the part-man, part-horse centaur (which first appears at Lefkandi *c.* 900) seems to be a purely Greek invention.

Continuity

Although the renewed contacts with the flourishing cultures of the Levant clearly had a profound impact on the rustic Greeks of the early Iron Age, we can also detect elements of the Mycenaean past which endured through those long dark centuries. Along with certain aspects of aristocratic society such as the war chariot and the value of metals, it is the warrior ethos that survives and plays a major role in later Greek culture. An overwhelming desire to be acclaimed the best (*aristos*), whether on the battlefield or in the stadium, permeates Greek literature and thought, and this competitive spirit is what impelled the Greeks to venture forth beyond the narrow and safe confines of their citadels both in the Bronze Age and later.

There is continuity as well in many other aspects which are part of later Greek identity. In terms of religion, several of the gods named on the Linear B tablets are the Olympians to whom temples began to be built *c.* 700 BC, temples which in their plans recall the megara of the Mycenaean palaces. The concept of kinship as exemplified by Bronze Age family burials and a related respect for

41 Bronze griffin head once attached to the rim of a cauldron, *c.* 650 BC. H. 23.4 cm. The curved base with attachment holes indicates that this hollow-cast bronze griffin was once attached to the shoulder of a bronze bowl. Its function was probably apotropaic, that is, to ward off evildoers from the sanctuary where it was dedicated.

42 Jug with a griffin-head spout. Cycladic, *c.* 675–650 BC. H. 41.5 cm. The spout on this ceramic jug may have been inspired by the popular bronze cauldron attachments and illustrates the Greeks' inventiveness in adapting foreign motifs to their own media.

43 Birth of Pandora. Campanian red-figure amphora, *c.* 450–425 BC. H. 30.8 cm. This quirkily decorated vase shows the creation of the first woman, Pandora, by the craftsman god Hephaistos. Called a 'beautiful evil' by Hesiod, she reputedly opened a pithos (not a pyxis or box as later authors have misunderstood the term) filled with evils, but it was capped by Zeus just before Elpis (Hope) could escape. On this side of the vase Elpis is the small head just emerging from the jar as Zeus looks on. A version of this story was also represented on the base of Pheidias' statue of Athena in the Parthenon.

ancestors (note the Grave Circle enclosing earlier Mycenaean shaft graves) were important means of asserting status in the later Iron Age. Likewise the feasting and drinking which took place among Homer's aristocracy continued among the wealthy throughout the 'Dark Age'.

Perhaps the figure who best exemplifies this age of iron is the poet who invented the term, Hesiod. In the opening of his hymn to Zeus known as *Works and Days* he outlines the races of man in chronological order as: gold, silver, bronze, heroes and iron. Whereas his predecessor Homer wrote about the age of heroes, Hesiod complains that he lives in that of iron, thus one of hardship, suffering and violence. His poem speaks in the first person and calls for justice as it dispenses moral teachings as well as practical advice for the farmer about when to plough and when to sow. Hesiod's other surviving hymn is dedicated to the Muses, whom he claims to have met on Mt Helikon near his farm in Boiotia. Entitled *Theogony*, it recounts in Genesis-like fashion the genealogies of all the gods, their battles for hegemony and the eventual triumph of Zeus. Both poems mention the creation of the first woman, Pandora, who, not unlike the biblical Eve, gives in to temptation and brings ruin to mankind. But despite Hesiod's grim outlook, things were definitely looking up in the Greek world as populations grew, cities multiplied, new leaders emerged, laws and constitutions were written, grand temples were constructed and the arts flourished.

4

Life in the Polis: A Man's World

44 Reconstructed aerial view of ancient Athens in the mid-fourth century BC. Drawing by Peter Connolly. The civic centre or Agora is situated in the centre of the city at lower left and is bordered by stoas; the fortified Acropolis with its monumental entrance and temples of Athena looms up in the centre. Connecting the two is the street known as the Panathenaic Way, which begins at one of the gates of the walled city and ends at the bottom of the wide ramp leading to the Acropolis. Just outside lies one of the major cemeteries, known as the Kerameikos. The city expanded over time and so the modest houses and workshops do not adhere to any regular plan as in other Greek cities.

According to Aristotle, 'men come together in the city to live; and they remain to live the good life'. The majority of Greek citizens lived 'the good life' in what they called a *polis* from the eighth century BC Roman times. Although the term *polis* originally signified simply a fortified place, it came to stand for an independent state consisting of a city and its immediate hinterland. Such city-states had long been a common form of political and social organization in the ancient Near East, but they were never so widespread nor as long-lasting as they were in Greek lands stretching from the Black Sea to North Africa, and from Spain to Afghanistan (following its conquest by Alexander). At any one time there were as many as a thousand such city-states arrayed along the shores of the Mediterranean, such that Greek settlements have been compared to frogs sitting around a pond. These *poleis* (plural) could range in size, from ten square km and a population of less than a thousand inhabitants to a megalopolis like Alexandria with its population estimated at half a million, but the ideal size was considered to be about 10,000 male citizens. In spite of the geographical expanse and demographic variety of these city-states, the Greeks who lived in them considered themselves one people. According to the historian Herodotos (8.144.3), there were four things that all Greeks had in common: ancestry, language, religion and customs.

For this reason an ancient Greek travelling the Mediterranean Sea would probably have felt at home in most of the city-states he encountered. He would normally arrive by ship since Greek cities were regularly situated on or near sheltered natural harbours. Typically the *polis* was still a fortified place, because most had a walled acropolis (literally a 'high city') to which the citizenry could retreat in times of attack as well as fortification walls surrounding the inhabited area. Just outside the walls were the cities' cemeteries, comprising private family plots filled with marble gravestones and public memorials to the war dead. Within the walls there would usually be an open, centrally located public space, know as the agora, often officially delimited by inscribed *horoi* or boundary stones. The agora was both a commercial and a civic centre and so here one encountered daily markets and the tables of money-changers along with various government buildings. These might include a *bouleuterion* (council house),

prytaneion (executive committee meeting hall), law courts, a *metroon* (official archives), and colonnaded stoas with rooms for public dining. Both the acropolis and the lower city accommodated a number of cult places, ranging from open-air altars to stone temples. Highly developed cities of the Classical period, such as Athens and Corinth, also featured buildings with specialized functions, such as fountain-houses, brothels, a mint and a prison. For entertainment and other public assemblies there was usually an open-air theatre set into a hillside, possibly an odeion or roofed concert hall, a gymnasium for exercise, a palaistra for wrestling, and a stadium or race track for athletic contests. Later Hellenistic cities boasted extensive libraries, market buildings, military barracks, and shrines of the healing god Asklepios which functioned as hospitals. Thus ancient Greek citizens had many of the amenities enjoyed by city dwellers today.

The geography of mainland Greece lent itself to a proliferation of these independent, self-governing city-states. Because the country is mostly mountainous with few large open valleys, *poleis* were isolated from one another. Those with excellent harbours such as Athens, Corinth, Syracuse and Miletos became more cosmopolitan and progressive through trade, shipping and the presence of foreigners. Landlocked and hence more remote places like Sparta and Thebes (Boiotia) tended to be more insular and conservative. Natural resources are not plentiful in Greece, and it is rarely that cities had mineral sources to exploit – the silver mines of Attika and gold mines of Siphnos being the exceptions. The island of Paros rose to prominence because of its exceptional white marble, and the islands of Samos, Thasos and Chios in the northern Aegean islands produced excellent wines which were widely exported, judging from their terracotta transport amphorae that are found far and wide. Some places, like the island of Aigina, had no natural resources but nevertheless became wealthy from shipping, a prominent Greek industry throughout history.

Coinage

The individuality and independence of these city-states are perhaps best represented by their great variety of coin types and weight standards. Each *polis* had its own readily identifiable medium of exchange, with the notable exception of Sparta which clung to its old-fashioned iron spits (*obeliskoi*) long after coinage has become almost universally accepted in the Classical period. The obol (from the word for the iron spit) continued to be the term used for a small denomination and *drachm* refers to a 'handful of them', that is, six obols. In the seventh century the idea of coinage was adapted from the Lydians of western Turkey whose king Kroisos ('as rich as Croesus') was legendary for his hoards of gold. Coinage came about when lumps of metal of a standard weight were

45 Two Greek coins. Top to bottom: Electrum stater of Phokaia, *c.* 600–550 BC. W. 16.518 g. Without any letters it is difficult to assign this early coin to a specific *polis*, though the seal may provide a clue. The Greek word for seal is *phoke* and so this coin was probably minted at Phokaia in Ionia before its citizens emigrated west in 540.

Below: Silver stater (= 2 drachms) of Aigina, late sixth century BC. W. 11.34 g. The famous silver coins of this Aegean island feature a turtle on one side and a punch mark on the other.

46 Two Greek coins. Top: Silver tetradrachm (= 4 drachms) of Athens, *c.* 480 BC. W. 16.64 g. The slogan 'owls to Athens' is the equivalent of 'coals to Newcastle' but it refers to the city's famous coinage. The small owl or *glaux* on the reverse is the bird associated with the goddess Athena because it dwells in the rocky crevices of the Acropolis in Athens.

Below: Silver decadrachm (= 10 drachms) of Syracuse, Sicily, *c.* 413 BC. Signed by the engraver Kimon. W. 43.36 g. One of the most impressive and artistic Greek coins ever minted is the late fifth-century silver decadrachm of the *nouveau riche* Sicilian city of Syracuse. It proudly displays the personification of the local freshwater spring named Arethusa, surrounded by dolphins, on one side, and a victorious charioteer crowned by Nike, the winged goddess of victory, on the other. It is even signed very subtly by the artist Kimon: the first two letters of his name are engraved on Arethusa's headband. It has been suggested that these impressive coins were minted in honour of the Syracusans' crushing defeat of the Athenians in 413 BC – and so served as a kind of commemorative medal like later European medallions.

stamped with a symbol which served to identify the source and guarantee the value. Like Lydian coinage the earliest Greek coins were minted from a natural alloy of gold and silver known as electrum and are rather lumpy in shape. Eventually coins took the disc form we still use today.

The obverse (or 'head') of these early coins bears an image which could be a *type parlant* ('talking design') meaning that it illustrates the name of the city (as in the rose of Rhodes, or the sickle-shaped harbour of Zankle in Sicily), or it advertises some distinctive product of the city such as the ear of barley on the coins of Metapontum in southern Italy. Another common coin image is the head of the city's patron deity (Athena on the coins of Athens), but it is not until the Hellenistic period that portraits of political leaders appeared on Greek coinage. The reverse ('tail') of the earlier coinage is a simple square punch, whose deep impression guaranteed that the coin was not plated or forged. Later the ethnic or abbreviation of the city's name was engraved on the reverse dye.

It is evident from coin hoards found throughout the Mediterranean that some Greek currencies enjoyed a wide circulation. One was the so-called 'turtles' of the island of Aigina, famed in the Archaic period for its shipping. Even more widely circulated were the 'owls' of Athens produced from the rich vein of silver found in the early fifth century in the mines at Laurion, at the southern tip of Attika, which could produce as much as 20 tons of silver (750 talents) per year. Although these silver coins look similar, they were minted on different weight standards. A testament to the Athenian coinage, and its purity and reliability, is the fact that centuries later Alexander the Great adopted the

Athenian standard for his coinage, as did the Persians. Surprisingly the Persians even minted coins with the same reverse as Athens, namely an owl and a sprig of olive, but the legend reads *basileus* meaning 'king' instead of *ton Athenaion* which translates 'of the Athenians'.

Although coinage obviously facilitated trade and exchange, it was probably originally invented to pay mercenaries because at first there were no smaller denominations. As a result of the different weight standards in use money-changers conducted a lively business in the various Greek market places. However banks did not exist until the Renaissance, and wealth, both personal and public, was stored in temples where it was under the protection of the gods. In Athens the officials in charge of the state treasury regularly set up inscribed marble stelae on the Acropolis detailing the monies received as tribute from their allies in the Delian League and monies spent on public buildings like temples.

What will a drachm buy you?

The currency values in fifth-century Athens were:
6 obols = 1 drachm = 4.32 g of silver
100 drachms = 1 mina = approx. 1 pound of silver
6000 drachms = 60 minas = 1 talent

A skilled workman earned one drachm per day for manual labour, so this silver coin with the head of Athens represents four days' wages.

With his earnings a worker could buy:
Daily measure of grain, a cheap prostitute or a ferry ride across the River Styx: 1 obol
Interest on a loan of 1 mina for one month: 1 drachm
1 large red-figure ceramic hydria: 3 drachms
1 workman's tunic (*exomis*) or 2 kotylai (½ litre) of honey: 10 drachms
1 silver phiale (libation bowl) to dedicate to Athena: 100 drachms

1 medium-priced slave: 150 drachms
1 woollen robe dyed purple: 300 drachms
1 high-priced hetaira or courtesan: 500 drachms
1 good-quality racehorse: 1200 drachms
Dowry for 1 daughter from a well-off family: 8000 drachms
Ode by Pindar to celebrate an athletic victory: 10,000 drachms

47 Athenian tetradrachm, *c.* 480 BC.

Economy

The main employer in ancient Greece was the city-state itself. In the sixth century when Greek *poleis* were often governed by tyrants, public works were conducted on a large scale. The tyrant of the island of Samos, Polykrates, undertook especially ambitious projects. One was a harbour mole to protect his fleet of 100 warships, while another was an aqueduct bringing water to the city tunnelled for a kilometre through a mountain by workers starting simultaneously from both ends. He also erected a colossal Ionic temple to the goddess Hera. The plan of this temple was the largest ever conceived in the Greek world; its stylobate measured 55 by 109 m, and had it been completed (which it never was) it would have had a double row of columns around all four sides. The fifth-century so-called Periklean building programme in Athens provided employment for a wide variety of workers including masons, sculptors, wax-modellers, woodcarvers, carpenters, sawyers, joiners, lathe-workers, painters, gilders and general labourers working under the direction of the architects and their assistants. Each city-state supplied and underwrote the salaries of its armies, navies, juries, religious and festival personnel, and those involved in construction of temples and civic buildings. However, in Athens wealthy individuals would often personally assume the costs of a trireme or warship for the navy or a theatrical production for the main festival of Dionysos, the City Dionysia. These voluntary 'taxes' on the part of the rich were known as liturgies and considerable prestige accrued to those who undertook them.

Supporting the citizens of the city-states was both a rural and an urban economy. In ancient Greece land ownership was virtually synonymous with citizenship in that only citizens could own agricultural property. Thus most citizens had small farms outside the city which they used for growing food crops and pasturing their domesticated animals, mostly sheep, which provided wool, and pigs and goats. The Mediterranean climate is characterized by hot, dry summers and mild, wet winters, so it is ideal for the cultivation of olives. Olive oil had a wide variety of uses, from perfume to heating, and it also fuelled the ubiquitous oil lamp. Other crops that grow well in this climate are grapes, wheat, barley, legumes, figs and nuts. Nonetheless, cities with large populations and little arable land, like Athens, had to import grain to feed their citizens.

In investigating smaller businesses conducted in the cities, we know the most about Athens where there are documents listing as many as 170 different occupations, ranging from *aleiptria* (masseuse) to *zeugotrophos* (teamster). One of the enterprises we understand relatively well is the ceramics industry. Clay and timber for firing were plentiful in most places, and pots were needed for cooking, dining, food storage, perfumes, official dry and liquid measures, and wine and oil transport. In the Archaic period nearly every region had its own distinctive style of pottery, which, unlike the earlier Geometric pottery, was

48 Above: Ploughing and sowing. Athenian black-figure
Siana cup assigned to the Burgon Group, *c.* 575–550 BC.
Diam. 26.5 cm. The main staples of the Greek diet were
wheat and barley, and ploughing and sowing took place
in the autumn after the first rainfall. Scenes of agriculture
are surprisingly rare in Greek art, so this vase painting
may be a reference to a ritual in honour of the grain
goddess Demeter, who is depicted on the other side.

49 Opposite: Olive harvest. Athenian black-figure
amphora attributed to the Antimenes Painter, *c.* 520 BC.
H. 40 cm. The autumn olive harvest was one of the
major events in the agricultural year. In an orchard,
abbreviated here to three olive trees, two older men are
beating the branches with long sticks. One of their young
assistants is gathering the fallen olives while a second has
climbed the tree to beat the higher limbs.

50 Right: Grave stele of the cobbler Xanthippos.
Athenian, marble, *c.* 420 BC. H. 83.75 cm. Identifiable by
the last he holds in his right hand, this elderly shoemaker
is accompanied by his two young daughters. He is seated
on the characteristic Greek chair known as the *klismos*.

51 Metalworking. Athenian
black-figure oinochoe,
c. 510–500 BC. H. 26 cm.
With his long tongs
an older craftsman is
removing a piece of metal
from a tall shaft furnace,
where he has heated it
preparatory to working
it on an anvil. His young
assistant is standing ready
with his hammer.

widely exported especially to the colonies and Etruria. Corinthian and Laconian vases seem to have been popular trade items in the early sixth century, but eventually the fine red-and-black figured Athenian wares displaced all other fabrics. Because many potters and painters signed their vases and trademarks were often incised on the undersides of vessels, it is possible to reconstruct some aspects of the pottery industry. The potters appear to have been the owners of the establishments, while the painters moved around, decorating pots for different workshops. These were small family-run businesses and sons often followed in their fathers' footsteps, as they did in other professions like marble sculpting or bronze casting. Some of the names, like Amasis (an Egyptian pharaoh) or Skythes ('the Scythian') suggest foreign workers. Known in Athens as metics, these resident aliens could become quite wealthy, but never held citizenship.

52 Ivory figurine of a hunchback slave. Hellenistic, *c.* first century BC. H. 10 cm. This depiction of a hunchback with Pott's disease is excruciatingly realistic. Such portrayals of extreme deformity only became common in the Hellenistic period.

Slavery

A significant proportion of the work force in ancient Greece consisted of slaves, of which two types can be distinguished: chattel slaves were the property of individual masters and mostly foreigners; community slaves were owned by the state and often indigenous, subjected peoples. Among the latter the helots of Sparta are the best known, but Syracuse, for instance, also enslaved part of its population. Sometimes referred to as serfs, these were fellow Greeks who worked the hinterland contributing around fifty percent of their produce to the state, thereby enabling the Spartans to devote all their energies to the military. Written sources indicate that at Athens a citizen could own as many as 1000 slaves which he would lease out for profit, notably as mine workers or as crews for the state triremes. Metics also owned slaves and one named Kephalos put 120 to work in his shield-making establishment. A slave in Athens typically was valued between 150 and 250 drachmas, with highly skilled slaves costing as much as 360 drachmas, or the equivalent of a year's salary for a skilled worker.

53 Gortyn Law Code.
The oldest extant European
code of laws is that
inscribed on the walls of
an early fifth-century BC
building in central Crete.
The Gortyn Law Code,
as it is known, deals with
issues of status, stating for
instance that a slave could
be more severely punished
than a citizen for the same
offence, but if unfairly
treated a slave had recourse
to the courts, even for
injuries perpetrated by
his master. Perhaps
surprisingly, if a male slave
married a free woman,
their children were free.

Different methods were employed to control this large slave population. The Spartans went so far as to declare the helots enemies of the state so that they could execute any rebels with impunity. In Athens the opposite approach was adopted, namely making it possible for productive and loyal slaves to buy or win their freedom – and many did. After the battle of Arginousai in 406, in which large numbers of Athenian slaves fought alongside their masters, they were not only freed but also granted citizenship. Many household slaves who served families loyally as nurses and tutors were honoured with marble gravestones and loving tributes to their service. Thus, there were varying degrees of servitude in ancient Greece but slavery was a fact of life, in spite of Homer's claim that a man loses his selfhood when 'the day of slavery' comes upon him.

Politics

Although best known for its development of democratic governance, Greece in fact hosted a wide variety of political systems. Some, like the dual hereditary kingship of Sparta, were unique, while others, like tyranny, were ubiquitous, especially in the sixth century. In essence there were three possible forms of government: the rule of one (monarchy or tyranny), the rule of the few (oligarchy or aristocracy) and the rule of the many (democracy). Whatever system was in operation the Greeks believed that the rule of law (*nomos*), based on longstanding custom and often unrecorded, was ultimately superior. They did, however, establish written laws at an early period, citizens regularly swore

Jury duty

The Athenians went to great lengths to ensure the impartiality of their juries and the complex procedure is described in their constitution. Rectangular tickets made of bronze were inscribed with the name of a potential juror, here 'Aristophon, son of Aristodemos of the deme of Kothokidai'. Just before a case was to be heard, potential jurors inserted their tickets into the appropriate slots, according to the letter on their tickets (here *gamma*), of the marble *kleroterion* that stood at the entrance to the law courts. The slots were arranged in columns and rows, and at the side was a tube into which black and white balls were poured at random. Those jurymen whose tickets were in rows opposite the white balls were selected for the trial, whereas those with black balls were dismissed. The tickets were issued by the state and so were marked as official property with the owl of Athena.

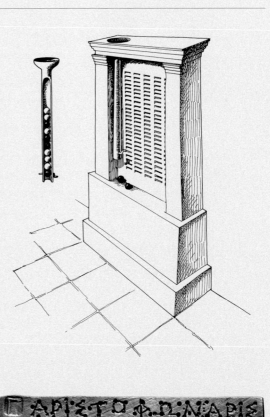

54 Drawing of a marble device known as a *kleroterion*.

55 Bronze juryman's ticket from Athens, mid-fourth century.

oaths to abide by their laws, and in theory the laws were upheld in people's courts. Lawgivers such as Solon of Athens became legendary; his laws were inscribed on wooden plaques and set up for public viewing.

In terms of real-life politics the work of government was carried out by magistracies composed of citizens rather than an entrenched bureaucracy. At Athens and elsewhere these consisted of boards of citizens appointed or chosen by lot for a year and not eligible for re-election to the same board. Because Athens was a fully participatory democracy (a Greek-derived term from *demos*/people and *kratos*/power), it developed elaborate mechanisms to ensure fairness and impartiality. Most magistrates were chosen by lot and juries were large, thus lessening the chance of bribery. Perikles instituted jury pay of two obols per day, and this cost to the state was not insignificant since juries could be

56 Portrait of Perikles. Roman copy of a Greek original of the late fifth century BC. H. 57.5 cm. Perikles was neither a king nor an elected ruler, but he held the position of 'general' for fifteen years. From 443 until his death in 429, he was highly successful in persuading the Assembly to pass his legislation, which included jury pay, a restriction on citizenship and an increase in the size of the cavalry.

as large as 500; however, trials never lasted more than a day. Speeches by prosecutors and defendants were rigorously timed with a simple device known as a water-clock, so when the prescribed amount of water drained out of the hole in the base of a clay pot, one's time was up.

With the exception of conservative Sparta, the politics of the *polis* were characterized by change and reform. In the sixth century tyrannies prevailed but the negative connotation of the term derives from Plato and Aristotle who considered it the worst form of government. Tyrants could be benevolent or malevolent, but they assumed their power by usurpation and with the backing of discontented citizens, rather than constitutionally. Tyrannies rarely lasted more than two generations, and were often replaced with a more democratic form of government. The classic example is again Athens, with the reforms instituted by Kleisthenes in 508. One of his innovations may have been ostracism, which was the official banishment for ten years of an individual who was deemed too powerful, that is, potentially a tyrant. Citizens voted for ostracism on sherds of pottery called *ostraka*. Kleisthenes' major reform was to divide the entire region of Attika into 139 municipalities or demes, which were then organized into ten tribes; each tribe sent fifty representatives to the new Council of 500 which prepared legislation for approval by the Assembly. This larger body consisted of all citizens, who by definition were males aged twenty and over, all of whom had a right to speak and vote with a show of hands. In the fourth century there were approximately 20,000 citizens and about 6000 of them usually showed up for the Assembly, which met forty times a year outdoors on the Pnyx, a broad low hill near the Acropolis.

'Know thyself'

As preparation for citizenship, which entailed military service as well as civic duties, most Greek states provided education for their young men. In wealthier families boys would grow up with a resident tutor (usually a family slave called a *paidagogos;* see Chapter 5, fig. 74 left), and at the age of seven would leave home to study with specialists in reading and writing, music and athletics. While the gymnasium was originally a place for physical exercise, it soon became an educational institution where philosophers set up shop. Plato established his philosophical school at a gymnasium outside the city known as the Academy, and Aristotle's was at a place called the Lyceum.

Philosophical and scientific thinking began with intellectuals in East Greece who used empirical reasoning as opposed to mythological explanations for the

57 Schoolboys. Athenian red-figure chous, attributed to the Shuvalov Painter, *c*. 425 BC. H. 15 cm. The seated youth holds an inscribed book roll while the younger boy is reciting, his lyre in hand. According to Plato, 'the *kitharistes* teaches the boys to play the lyre and then to sing lyric songs to their own accompaniment. In this way they become more cultured, more controlled and better balanced people, and their behaviour is all the better for it.'

study of natural phenomena. Many, like Thales of Miletos (*c*. 575 BC), sought to define the basic essence of the material world. For him this was water, because it was the only substance that could exist in three forms as a liquid, solid and gas, but for his fellow Milesian Anaximenes it was air, because it could oscillate between the extremes of hot and cold. For the followers of the mathematician Pythagoras, who lived in southern Italy, 'all things are number'. Demokritos, the most famous of the later fifth-century atomists, proposed an infinite number of invisible particles making up matter, namely the atom which means 'that which cannot be cut'. All these pre-Sokratic philosophers, as they are known, sought logical explanations for how the world was organized and used elements of logic to reach their conclusions. They thereby laid the groundwork for much of later Western philosophy.

58 Portrait statuette of Sokrates (*c.* 470–399 BC), Hellenistic. H. 27.5 cm. After Sokrates' execution in 399, the Athenians, full of remorse, commissioned the famous sculptor Lysippos to make a portrait statue of the philosopher to be set up near the gates to the city. This small statuette may be a copy of that portrait.

59 Portrait of Antisthenes, founder of the Cynic school of philosophy. Roman copy of Greek original of *c.* 300 BC. H. 38 cm. Antisthenes, a devoted follower of Sokrates, opened his own school of philosophy known as the Cynics. He has the appearance of the typical dishevelled philosopher as described by Lucian: 'a halo of beard, eyebrows an inch above their place, superiority in his air, a look that might storm heavens, locks waving in the wind – a very Boreas or Triton from Zeuxis' brush.'

It was not until the late fifth century that Athens achieved its fame as a place of learning. Attic philosophers were less interested in the physical world than in moral virtue and the rights and obligations of individuals and society at large. The earliest, Sokrates (*c.* 470–399 BC), had no establishment but simply wandered the city, teaching young men in public buildings or shops. He appears to have written nothing, but his dialogues were recorded by his pupils of whom the most famous were Plato and Xenophon. He conducted his dialogues on ethics and truth using what we now call the Socratic Method, whereby he led his questioners to contradict themselves. Because of his habit of questioning everything, he was eventually charged with impiety or disrespect for the gods, convicted, and forced to take his own life with a dose of lethal hemlock. His closest follower Plato (428–347) proposed the existence of ideal forms of which worldly phenomena are mere shadows; because philosophers came closest to recognizing these ideals, in his opinion they were the best suited to rule. Although Aristotle (384–322) studied under Plato, his philosophy was grounded in the real world and he ambitiously attempted to systematize all knowledge including science. Two further popular but opposing schools of philosophy were the Cynics, who preached 'live according to nature', that is simply, and the Epicureans, who espoused the belief that pleasure is the object of human life, with the proviso that too much pleasure can cause pain.

While Athenian youths were engaged in friendly wrestling bouts in the palaistra and debating the purpose of life in the shade of the Academy, Spartan boys were being drilled in a militaristic and totalitarian system of education that was single-mindedly designed to produce the finest soldiers. From the age of seven every Spartiate underwent an austere upbringing, living in a barracks under the control of the state, dining in a common mess, and devoting most of his time to physical training. The system resulted in an extremely unified and uniform citizen body who called themselves *homoioi* or peers, as opposed to equals. The Spartan code was best exemplified during their legendary, though ultimately unsuccessful, stand at the narrow pass of Thermopylai in 480 when for four days they held the massive Persian army at bay. Dying to a man, King Leonidas and his 300 troops fulfilled the Spartan mother's command to her son: 'Come back with your shield or on it'.

Warfare

One negative consequence of the competitive *polis* system was that Greek states were almost constantly at war, at loggerheads with each other over their borders, their control over other *poleis* and sanctuaries, or even perceived insults to their honour. During the Classical period it has been estimated that Athens was at war in two years out three. The theme of battle permeated all aspects of life – the

60 Rhodian plate with Menelaos and Hektor fighting over the body of Euphorbos, *c.* 600 BC. Diam. 38 cm. Although the scene is mythological, these warriors are equipped with the full hoplite panoply: crested helmets, short thrusting spears, round shields or *hopla*, corselets and greaves. Hoplites were obliged to provide not only their own armour but also their rations and bedding.

71

61 Epitaph for the Athenian casualties at Potidaia, 432 BC. H. 30 cm, W. 34.5 cm. The Athenians under the leadership of the general Kallias fought and won a battle against Potidaia in the northern Aegean just before the outbreak of the Peloponnesian War in 432. A memorial was set up in Athens to commemorate the war dead, which reads: 'The air received the spirits and the earth the bodies of these men undone around the gates of Potidaia; of their enemies some attained the destiny of the grave, others fled and made the wall their surest hope [of life]. This city and the people of Erechtheus mourn the men who died in battle before Potidaia, sons of Athenians, placing their lives in exchange for glory and bringing honour to their native land.'

imagery of temples and wall paintings, the tragedies performed in the theatre, the songs sung at symposia, the speeches delivered to the assembly, and most poignantly in the funeral orations for the war dead recited in the state cemeteries. The actual wars themselves were more like skirmishes, brief incursions into an enemy's territory, some pillaging and ravaging of the countryside, an engagement with the enemy – akin to a pushing match – until one side threw down its heavy shields and fled. The victors stripped the enemy corpses of their armour and set up a temporary trophy at the point where the battle turned. A truce would be called, so that bodies could be retrieved from the battlefield for burial at home.

With the exception of Sparta and Thebes, most city-states had no standing armies, but called up amateur militias as needed. In principle a citizen was required to be ready for active duty between the ages of eighteen and fifty-nine, and he received no formal combat training or pay. The hoplite was the military and social ideal, and the Greeks generally had little regard for those who served in the cavalry and navy because they did not engage in fierce face-to-face combat and were, like mercenaries, paid for their services. Nonetheless Athens' navy played a decisive role in defeating the Persians in 479 when its swift, highly manoeuvrable triremes succeeded in trapping the large, cumbersome Persian ships in the Bay of Salamis and decimated them with their ramming tactics. Because of the expense of maintaining horses and the lack of open spaces in which to exercise them, the cavalry did not develop until later and was used mostly to attack the invading armies ravaging one's countryside.

The great military innovation of the Archaic period was the phalanx wherein coordinated movement was as essential as bodily strength. The heavy infantrymen, whose armour could weigh over 22 kg, marched in formation so

62 Two Greek ships. Athenian black-figure kylix attributed to the Leagros Group, *c.* 510 BC. Diam. 20 cm. The prow of a deep-bellied merchant ship at the left is about to be rammed by an oared galley at the right. Note the long boar's snout, made of bronze, at the prow of the man-o'-war. Piracy was very common in the ancient Mediterranean and even at times considered a respectable way of earning a living.

that the shield carried on the hoplite's left arm helped to protect the exposed right flank of his comrade. The Greek phalanx however was no match for the later Macedonian phalanx, which was developed and intensively trained by Philip II in the mid-fourth century. These professional, full-time soldiers fought in a tighter formation, typically sixteen rows deep, with smaller shields and exceptionally long spears which made penetration all but impossible. A new piece of siege equipment also enabled Philip of Macedon's success. The catapult was first used by the Syracusans in 397, but it was Philip who realized its potential by adding tightly twisted ropes to create torsion, thus propelling massive stones and arrows over considerable distances.

The symposium: wine, women, song … and boys

Besides warfare one of the most important institutions of male life in ancient Greece was the symposium. Symposia had been an essential part of the lifestyle of the elite for centuries, and these drinking parties are often depicted on Greek pottery, much of which was used for the service and consumption of wine. The symposium was held in a special room of the house called an *andron* (literally men's room) which was set up with wooden couches fitted with cushions where the banqueters, usually two to a couch, reclined on their left elbows. After the meal, wine which had been diluted with water was served from a large krater or mixing bowl into stemmed bowls called kylixes. These cups were often used for

63 Entertainment at the symposium. Athenian red-figure cup attributed to the Brygos Painter, *c.* 490–480 BC. Diam. 31.9 cm. A young girl, probably a slave (denoted by her short hair) is dancing before a youth stretched out on his banqueting couch. He holds a wind instrument in his hands and a deep wine cup rests on the table next to him. Both he and the girl are wearing festive wreaths, hallmarks of the symposium.

64 Satyr play at the symposium. Athenian red-figure psykter (wine cooler) attributed to Douris, *c.* 490 BC. H. 28 cm. This vase, a specialized shape for cooling wine, was placed in a krater filled with cold water. Appropriately its decoration consists of playful satyrs, followers of the wine god Dionysos. Here one performs a superhuman feat with his wine vessel.

65 Bronze reclining banqueter, probably Spartan, *c.* 530–500 BC. L. 10 cm. The Spartans partook of special symposia called *syssitia* which were more like a soldier's mess. These *syssitia* helped in the creation of a unified citizenry committed to the goals of the militaristic state.

a drinking game known as *kottabos* in which the dregs of the wine were flipped out toward a metal target on a stand. Prayers and toasts were offered at the beginning of every symposium and music and conversation followed; entertainment was often provided by girl dancers and flute players, hired for the evening, and the revelling often ended in drunkenness and sex, both hetero- and homosexual.

One of Sokrates' most famous dialogues is entitled the *Symposium*, for it uniquely takes place at one of these all-night, all-male drinking parties. As recorded by Plato, the topic of discussion was love, which the philosopher defined as a quest for the Beautiful and the Good rather than sexual gratification. Also attending this symposium was a *kalos k'agathos* ('good and beautiful') Athenian youth named Alkibiades, a pupil of Sokrates, whose physical charms did not tempt the older man. It was normal in much of Greek society for an older man to be physically attracted to an adolescent and to gratify his desire in a homoerotic relationship in which the youth played the passive role. The mythological model was Zeus' attraction to the Trojan prince Ganymede whom he abducted to Mt Olympos. These unions were not exclusive, for mortal men, like Zeus, also had wives and concubines. We turn now to the 'distaff side' to examine the lives of women and the Greek household.

5

Life in the Oikos:
The Greek Household

66 Opposite: Athenian woman spinning. White-ground jug (oinochoe) attributed to the Brygos Painter, *c.* 490 BC. H. 21.5 cm. Spinning was one of the principal activities of Greek women, and this delicate drawing on a wine jug may be the finest extant portrayal. A young woman holds up in her left hand the distaff covered with clumps of red wool, from which she twists a thread with her right hand. The thread is attached to the spindle which has almost reached the ground, at which point she will stop and wind the thread around it. The white background of this vase is a special technique which Athenian potters eventually used only for funerary vessels, many of which feature women visiting the cemetery (see fig. 83).

Whereas the male-dominated agora was the centre of public activity in ancient Greece, the house or *oikos* was the locus of private life and the domain of women. The Greek word *oikos*, however, means more than our word 'house' and is better translated as 'household', because the *oikos* not only incorporated the domestic activities of women and children but also served as an economic enterprise, often based on slave labour. And at least in Athens, where we have the most written evidence for the workings of the Greek household, the *oikos* functioned importantly as a true sub-unit of the state or *polis*. It usually incorporated three generations: the male head and his wife and children, as well as his parents and household slaves. The patriarch ruled the *oikos*, determining for example whether a newborn child would be allowed to live or be left exposed to die because of defects or gender. Female babies were sometimes abandoned as they were considered too expensive to bring up.

In this chapter we turn our focus to the lives of women, both those incorporated into citizen households and those who worked outside it. In the past few decades feminist scholarship has raised as many issues in this area as it has answered questions about life in ancient Greece. Were women severely constrained from appearing in public? Were they utterly powerless or did some areas such as religious observance and cult activity offer them a form of agency and authority? Women played key roles in the life cycle through the various rites of passage from birth to death. Let us begin with the physical setting where the activities of daily life took place.

Hearth and home

In contrast to later Hellenistic and Roman houses, Greek domestic architecture of the sixth to the fourth centuries was fairly modest. Useful evidence for houses and their contents comes from the northern Greek site of Olynthos which was totally destroyed by Philip II of Macedon in 348 BC, but its plan is well preserved. In this grid-plan city there were ten houses to each city block, and over 100 houses have been excavated. The building materials usually consisted of stone for the foundations, mud brick for the walls, and terracotta tiles for the roof. The floor plan was relatively small (the average area of a house at Olynthos is

67 Men reclining in the *andron*. Athenian red-figure cup, *c.* 480 BC. Diam. 31.5 cm. The outside of this drinking cup shows two couches end to end and a third at right angles to them, thus suggesting the layout of the *andron*, or men's dining room, where the couches were arrayed along the four walls. Low three-legged tables and cups hanging on the wall complete the symposium furnishings.

about 240 sq m) and enclosed, with blank walls to the exterior. Life was centred around an open courtyard which provided light and fresh air to the interior. Rooms were aligned along the north side in order to take advantage of southern exposure, while assuring greater warmth in the winter. Based on the writings of the Roman architectural historian Vitruvius, two types of house can be distinguished: those with a long loggia along the courtyard, known as the *pastas* house, and those with a two-columned porch leading to the main room, called the *prostas* type. These covered areas provided protection from the sun in summer within the courtyard where many domestic activities took place. Occasionally there were also upstairs rooms as indicated by the lower stone threshold blocks for wooden staircases which have long since disappeared.

It is not always easy to determine the function of specific rooms in a Greek house, but one obvious clue is the off-centre doorway. This feature allowed for the placement, end-to-end, of seven or fifteen banquet couches for the all-male symposium discussed earlier. Interior decoration was minimal, if there was any at all. Some walls were painted in solid colours, and special rooms like the *andron* might be embellished with mosaic floors. Furnishings were also sparse. The most elaborate item of furniture was probably the banquet couch, which in the Hellenistic period had lavish bronze attachments. Multi-functional, it also served as a bed and eventually as one's bier. Simple stools must have been fairly

68 Woman dining. Athenian red-figure pyxis, *c.* 480 BC. In contrast to men, who reclined on couches when dining, women appear to have eaten alone in the women's quarters, seated on stools.

69 Woman with slave. Athenian red-figure skyphos, *c.* 470–460 BC. H. 15.3 cm. While the matron of the house sneaks a sip of wine, her slave attendant follows behind, laden down with a heavy wine skin and a jug.

ubiquitous if the evidence from vase painting is reliable, and the *klismos* or chair with a back (see Chapter 4, fig. 50) seems to have been a status symbol for well-to-do women. Clothes were folded and kept in wooden chests; in fact the evidence of press folds – what we might consider wrinkles – on one's garments was actually a sign of wealth because it implied that a person had a change of wardrobe. Other accoutrements of upper-class houses were lighting fixtures such as bronze stands for holding clay oil lamps, portable braziers for heat, and mirrors supported by standing females known as caryatid mirrors.

70 Women working wool. Athenian black-figure epinetron, *c.* 500–480 BC. L. 31.1 cm. In shape this ceramic object resembles a terracotta cover tile used on roofs. However, it is a piece of domestic equipment which served to cover a woman's thigh. The rough upper surface was used for preparing wool, an activity pursued by the women painted along the side.

71 Caryatid mirror. Corinthian, *c.* 460 BC. H. 42.5 cm. A woman serving as a support is known as a caryatid, hence the name of this type of mirror. The highly polished or silvered disc served as a reflective surface. The woman wears a belted woolen dress known as a *peplos*.

72 Fish plate. Campanian, *c.* 360–330 BC. Diam. 24.2 cm. This special-purpose plate is one of hundreds produced in southern Italy in the fourth century and placed in tombs. Swimming over its flat surface are a cuttlefish, rainbow wrasse and torpedo. There is a small central depression for the fish sauce.

A clue to the activities that went on in Greek households is provided by the many domestic items that were broken and relegated to refuse pits or discarded in wells after the household went out of use. There was clearly a great deal of specialized kitchen ware, comprising coarse, undecorated pottery used for grinding (mortars), cooking (pots and stands), baking (ovens), grilling (spit holders) as well as storage of food (pithoi) and wine (amphorae). Beekeeping is documented by the cylindrical terracotta beehives littering the sites of ancient farms in the countryside. Other clay objects frequently found in domestic contexts are spindle whorls, used in the spinning of wool, and pyramidal and disc-shaped loomweights. While the wooden warp-weighted looms themselves do not survive, depictions of looms on painted vases and the presence of loomweights document the activity of weaving, which was no doubt practised in every household since clothing and bedding were normally made by women at home. Thus raw materials, such as grain and wool, were brought into the *oikos* and processed by the women and slaves, for domestic use and possibly also for sale in the case of textiles.

The Greeks had two categories of food: staple or simple food known as *sitos*, and *opson* which was the accompaniment or relish. *Sitos* was cereals, such as barley made into porridge and wheat baked into loaves or cakes, which formed the bulk of the ancient diet. Legumes including chick peas and lentils were also consumed. Cheese, game and pickled or salted fish constituted *opson*, which was eaten in much smaller quantities. Fresh fish was one of the most expensive luxury foods. In southern Italy special plates were made for it – that is, unless they are simply objects produced for the grave to show off one's wealth.

73 Baby sitting in a potty chair. Athenian red-figured chous (miniature wine jug), *c.* 440–430 BC. H. 11 cm. Here a toddler sits in his special chair, shaking his rattle as if demanding attention. Or is he signalling that he has finished using his potty? Actual examples of ceramic infant chairs have been excavated in the Athenian Agora, but they date from an earlier period.

Butchered meat from domesticated animals was reserved for religious festivals and was mostly consumed in stews. Honey was the common sweetener, and fruits such as figs, grapes and apples were also cultivated. Olive oil served as the main source of fat, butter being considered the mark of a barbarian. The primary beverage was wine and it was drunk in large quantities by both adults and children, as it was considered healthier than water.

Birth and childhood

In ancient Athens birth notices were posted on the door of the house: a tuft of wool for a girl baby and an olive wreath for a boy. Already these symbols signalled the family's aspirations for their children, namely that the girl would grow up to become a paragon of domesticity, and the boy would earn his 'laurels' through athletic, military and/or civic accomplishments. These gender differences persisted throughout life in most Greek *poleis* (with the notable exception of Sparta) with young girls being trained in domestic arts in the home and boys receiving external schooling. Adolescent brides were secluded in their new abodes while young men joined the military. Finally, as mothers, women tended the household while their husbands carried out their civic duties in the agora. The ancient historian Xenophon states it succinctly: 'it is fitting that a woman should remain inside and not venture out of doors; but for a man to stay indoors and not attend to the work outside the house is disgraceful'.

Childbirth took place at home with the assistance of a midwife, who also purified the premises which were considered polluted, just as they were when a death occurred. A newborn was not given a name until ten days after birth, presumably because of the high infant mortality rate and the Greeks' habit of exposing sickly or deformed babies who were deemed unfit to live – as determined by the head of the household in Athens, and by the council of elders in Sparta. At Athens within one year of their birth, male children were enrolled in their fathers' *phratries*, age-old hereditary brotherhoods of all male citizens, in a public ceremony at which an oath was sworn proclaiming their legitimacy. Athenian children were also officially welcomed into the community at the

74 Two terracotta figurines representing caretakers. Boy with his *paidagogos* (male tutor), *c.* 375–350 BC. H. 11.5 cm. Old nurse holding a baby, *c.* 300 BC. H. 13.5 cm. In wealthy homes children may have had closer attachments to the family slaves than to their blood relations. If artistic representations can be relied upon, the old nurse tended the youngest children while the male tutor looked after the young boys.

Anthesteria, a spring festival celebrated in honour of the wine god Dionysos. They were given their first taste of the new wine in miniature jugs known as *choes* which are decorated with charmingly realistic images of young children at play. They also enjoyed a wide array of toys similar to ours (dolls, yo-yos, tops, carts, hoops), many of which have been found in children's graves, as well as pet birds, monkeys, cheetahs and dogs.

In wealthier Greek households the children were cared for by family servants, and often their closest familiars were wet nurses and household slaves. In the *Odyssey*, for instance, when the hero finally reaches home, it is not his wife Penelope who recognizes him after twenty years, but rather his aged nurse Eurykleia. Male servants often acted as tutors or *paidagogoi* for the boys of the household. At about the age of seven the boys, accompanied by their *paidagogoi*, went outside the home to more specialized teachers of reading and writing, music and athletics. Just as the hero Achilles both played the lyre and excelled at running, so Greek boys were trained to have sound minds in strong bodies.

Girls, on the other hand, remained at home until marriage at about the age of fifteen. Here they were taught the arts of textile making, spinning wool, weaving at the loom, and preparing food. The only occasions in Athens when

75 Boys playing with their carts. Athenian red-figured chous, *c.* 420–400 BC. H. 5.6 cm. These small-scale replicas of the standard Athenian wine measure (chous) were made for children during the annual wine festival of Dionysos. They are often found in children's graves and the decoration gives us a glimpse of the toys, games and pets they enjoyed during their lifetimes. Note the little wine jugs placed on either side of the boys.

young unmarried women ventured outside the *oikos* were to participate in religious festivals, as we see on the east frieze of the Parthenon where they served at the Panathenaic festival of Athena, and perhaps to fetch water at the fountain-house or sacred spring. Evidence for the latter comes from a series of late sixth-century Athenian water jars that show women equipped with hydrias conversing at the fountain-house. Their elaborate dress suggests that they are wives and daughters of citizens, though the inscribed names seem to refer to *hetairai* or prostitutes. Some scholars believe that carrying water was a lowly job that only slaves performed. Thus, these and other vase paintings provide often controversial evidence of women's lives in Athens.

76 Women at the fountain-house. Athenian black-figure hydria, *c.* 510 BC. H. 50.6 cm. One of the few occasions on which women left the home was to fetch water at the fountain-house. However, we do not know whether the women represented on these water vessels are the wives of citizens or their household slaves.

Do Greek girls go to school?

On the interior of this wine cup are two girls, one grabbing the other by her wrist and leading her away. Because the girl being led carries a tablet and stylus, scholars originally thought that they were going off to school, just as we often see boys doing. However this scene is unique, and so a second interpretation reads the vase as a symposium joke because Athenian girls don't really go to school. This reading may be confirmed by the scenes on the outside which pair off women in twosomes that recall the common depictions of older men courting youths. So, both scenes are parodies of male behaviour here enacted by females. A third identification is also possible. Might these be Spartan girls who actually were educated and who were known to have lesbian relationships? This vase demonstrates the difficulty of interpreting unusual scenes of women in Athenian vase painting.

77 Athenian red-figure kylix attributed to the Painter of Bologna 417, *c.* 460 BC. Diam. 36.5 cm.

Although Spartan girls took physical exercise in order to make themselves stronger mothers who would bear healthy children, there is little evidence that Athenian or other Greek girls did much in the way of physical activity. While there are numerous vase paintings of boys at school and in the gymnasium, the only girls receiving instruction seem to be young dancers. Given their nudity or short tunics, they were clearly not daughters of citizens but rather entertainers at the all-male symposium, as seen earlier. This class of females also provided musical entertainment in the form of flute playing, and were highly paid to do so. *Hetairai* were high-class, often foreign-born, educated courtesans, not unlike the geishas of Japan; a notable example is Aspasia, the mistress of Perikles, whom he eventually married. At the other extreme were common streetwalkers known as *pornai* (whence our term pornography) and household slaves who were forced to serve their masters' whims. Many *hetairai* amassed enough wealth to make lavish dedications at Greek sanctuaries. Phryne, for instance, the mistress of the sculptor Praxiteles, dedicated a gold portrait of herself at Delphi.

Dress and nudity

One of the surest ways of determining whether a female depicted in Greek art was a respectable woman or a *hetaira* seems to be her dress or lack thereof. Thus, nude or scantily dressed women (with the exception of the goddess Aphrodite beginning in the mid-fourth century) are usually to be identified as prostitutes and fully draped women as citizen wives and daughters. We do not deduce from this that 'working' women wore no clothes, just as we do not believe that males fought in the nude, even though Greek art is replete with naked warriors. Nudity is a form of 'dress', that is, an artistic convention that helps the viewer better comprehend roles, just as size is often an indication of status, as when the gods are shown larger than humans or slaves much smaller than their masters. The situation is rather more complex than this for not all prostitutes are depicted nude, nor are all nude women prostitutes, and there are many manifestations of male nudity, from the servile to the divine.

Dress, however, is also an important indicator of status in Greek art and life. Unfortunately almost all textiles are lost because over time they disintegrate in the fluctuating climate conditions of Greece, in contrast to Egypt where the dry conditions promote preservation. Hence we must turn to artistic representations to understand what clothes were worn and what they signified. Male citizens of the leisure class wore a large woollen cloak known as a himation,

78 Youth playing flute as a *hetaira* dances. Athenian red-figured cup signed by Epiktetos, *c.* 500 BC. Diam. 32.5 cm. As the youth plays the aulos (flute), his female companion dances with her castanets. Her nudity indicates her status as a *hetaira*, and the animal skin flung around her torso suggests her untamed nature.

79 Marble grave stele of a youth, *c.* 350 BC. H. 1.94 m. The deceased is the idealized nude youth at the right, shown as an athlete. He is being offered an oil flask by his attendant or slave, who is portrayed as a smaller although not necessarily younger figure.

a somewhat impractical garment because one needed free hands to hold it in place. Working men wore more practical dress, a short belted tunic often with one shoulder bare in order to free the arms for physical labour. Travellers wear short cloaks and caps, usually the broad rimmed sun hat or *petasos*. Women are shown in long, tubular dresses, either of linen (chiton) or wool (peplos). The chiton has buttoned sleeves, but the peplos was clasped at the shoulders with long metal stick pins or fibulae, which resemble cloth nappy pins. Over this was worn a heavy woollen mantle, and sometimes a head veil, snood or a hairnet. On their feet both men and women wore sandals or short leather boots. Brides may have received their first pair of shoes upon leaving home to join the household of their new husband.

Marriage and family

In most ancient societies marriage was an economic and contractual pact arranged by the male kinsmen of the future bride and groom and Greece was no exception. The girl's father had to provide a dowry consisting of cash and moveable property, and she in turn was supported for life by her future husband's family. If there was no male heir in a family, a daughter could be married to her cousin or uncle in order to keep property within the clan. The primary purpose of marriage was to provide legitimate offspring, preferable male, and a girl did not become known as a woman (*gyne*) until she had done so. A woman's inability to produce children was grounds for divorce.

Wedding ceremonies are depicted on a number of Athenian vases, especially those manufactured for women. The bride is usually portrayed heavily veiled and being led to her new home by the groom, his hand leading her by the wrist. The procession took place at night with the mother and mother-in-law of the bride bearing torches. A young boy, stipulated as having both parents still living, accompanied the procession, as a fertility charm for the new couple. Although typically the groom was twice the age of his bride, around thirty, he is often unrealistically shown on these vases as a handsome youth. Family scenes, on the other hand, are extremely rare, perhaps because fathers were seldom seen in the *oikos*, except at night, and may have had little interaction with the women and children of the household. In Classical Athens, for which we have the most evidence, the average age of death for males was forty-five, while that for females was thirty-six, since many died in childbirth. Thus most children grew up orphaned of at least one of their parents.

80 An Athenian wedding. Athenian red-figure pyxis attributed to the Marlay Painter, *c.* 430 BC. Diam. 12.4 cm. In a typical wedding procession the groom leads his bride by the wrist to her new abode, where she is received by her mother-in-law. Here the idealized couple are transported by chariot.

81 The Greek family (?). Athenian red-figured pelike, *c.* 430–420 BC. H. 18.5 cm. Family scenes are quite rare in Greek vase painting, and this image of a child crawling towards its mother is unique. Men were seldom involved in child rearing, so the man at the left could be the child's *paidagogos* (tutor) rather than his father.

Festivals and funerals

From a fairly young age, perhaps seven, some aristocratic girls took part in religious rituals and public festivals. The most common role was as a member of a girls' chorus in which songs and dances were performed for deities. Some activities are seen as coming of age rites, like the girls' foot race in honour of Hera at Olympia or a similar event held in the Attic countryside (Brauron) for the goddess Artemis. Older maidens on the verge of marriage bore the sacred basket (*kanoun*) at the head of sacrificial processions. These females are particularly prominent on the Parthenon frieze, as is the priestess of Athena just over the doorway to the temple (see Chapter 6, p. 101, fig. 93).

There was no priesthood or official training for religious personnel in ancient Greece; they were simply ordinary citizens who served for a term, or sometimes life, and carried out the duties pertaining to particular cults. Often the position of priestess (or priest) was a hereditary one held and jealously guarded by older, aristocratic families. Rather different was the priestess, or Pythia as she was known, of the oracle of Apollo at Delphi. First, unlike most priestesses, she served a male deity, and her only duty was to utter unintelligible pronouncements which were then interpreted by the priests for the petitioners. Regular priestesses had a variety of functions from dressing and cleaning cult statues to overseeing sacrifices. Their concierge function was symbolized by the attribute they are often shown with, a key, which they used to lock and unlock the temple.

Death is the other realm in which women played significant roles, probably because it was deemed polluting, like childbirth. The significance of a proper burial in the ancient Greek world is powerfully demonstrated in Sophokles' tragedy *Antigone*, first performed in 442 BC. The protagonist of the play insists on burying her brother in spite of King Kreon's order to the contrary; she believes that the natural law which prescribes proper burial supersedes the law of the state and her defiant act of civil disobedience eventually results in her own death, and the belated acknowledgement by the king that he has erred disastrously. The Greeks went to elaborate lengths to retrieve corpses from the battlefield, to offer propitiatory rites for those who died at sea and so were unburied, and to ensure that the bones of their heroes were inhumed in local shrines so that they could receive regular homage and protect the *polis*.

It was the job of the women of the deceased's family to prepare the corpse for burial. The body was washed, wrapped in a funeral shroud, and laid out on a bier, its head propped on a pillow or tied with a string so the jaw would not gape open. After a period of mourning by men, women and children, the body was

82 Portrait of an old woman, possibly the priestess Lysimache. Roman copy of a Greek bronze original, three-quarter life-size, of the late fifth century BC. H. 30 cm. Pliny mentions a statue of a priestess of Athena named Lysimache who served the goddess for sixty-four years, and a base with her name possibly inscribed on it was found on the Athenian Acropolis. This priestess may be the model for the lead character in Aristophanes' comedy *Lysistrata*.

carried on a cart to the cemetery where it was either inhumed in a stone-lined cist grave, or cremated with the bones and ashes placed in a burial urn in the ground. Grave goods were usually modest, a few oil flasks and some personal possessions such as jewellery and mirrors for women or weapons and armour for men. Eventually a marker such as a marble stele, or an urn in the shape of an enlarged oil lekythos or loutrophoros (a type of nuptial water vessel) for an unmarried woman, was set up over the grave, inscribed with the name of the deceased.

The painted imagery on the white-ground oil flasks (*lekythoi*) deposited in Attic and neighbouring graves illustrates important practices and beliefs relating to death, such as the idea that a hoary ferryman named Charon rowed the souls of the dead to the other side of the River Styx. These painted vases also attest to periodic visits to the grave on the part of (mostly) female members of the family who regularly adorned the grave stele with ribbons, set wreaths and perfume vessels on its steps, and mourned the passing of their relations. That women could get carried away in their demonstrations of grief is indicated by special legislation limiting the number of mourners and restricting them to close relatives.

The circumscribed lives of Greek women are of course not unusual in antiquity, or in fact in certain regions of the world today. Legally they were considered minors, politically they had no citizenship rights, and socially they were kept out of sight. The only public recognition of women was on their gravestones, where they were praised for being good mothers and loyal wives. In a speech of Perikles as recorded by Thucydides, a woman's virtue was her invisibility, 'not to be spoken of whether in praise or blame'.

83 Woman attending a tomb. Athenian white-ground lekythos, *c.* 460 BC. H. 30 cm. This vase, of a type used in Greek funerals, appropriately depicts a woman visiting the grave of a deceased family member. Set on the stepped base of the stele are a large lekythos and another perfume vessel, to which the woman will add the alabastron in her right hand.

6

Religions, Gods and Heroes

In many ways the magnificent sculptures carved for the mid-fifth century Temple of Athena Parthenos on the Acropolis of Athens neatly sum up the essence of Greek religion. The twelve Olympian gods play a starring role. They are the largest and most prominently placed figures on the east side, appearing in all three sculpted areas, the pediment, metopes and frieze, thus highlighting their centrality in Greek cult. Heroes rank second, figuring primarily in the high-relief metopes along the other sides of the building, illustrating their importance in the mythological past. Finally the human adherents form a low relief procession subtly placed behind the colonnade, leading the victims for the central act of worship, animal sacrifice. This festive procession is accompanied by musicians playing flute and lyre and women carrying equipment for fumigation (incense burners) and liquid libations (phialai and oinochoai). Cult personnel consist of a citizen priest and priestess, who are preoccupied with a votive offering for the divinity. Most splendid of all and positioned at the rear of the central room (cella) of the temple stood a colossal cult image, with a reflecting pool of water in front to enhance the gleam of the statue's golden drapery.

While more lavish than most sanctuaries, the Acropolis incorporates all the elements of a typical Greek temenos: walled perimeter, gated entry, open-air altar, stone temple(s) housing a likeness of a deity, and votive offerings of all types and materials from modest inscribed vases to costly over life-size statues. Greek religion was conservative and changed little over time, although new divinities were admitted to the pantheon and festivals added to the religious calendar. Unlike the major religions of today, Greek religion was polytheistic, had no sacred text such as the Bible or Koran, and lacked a professional clergy. It consisted mostly of ritual acts performed in honour of various deities and in anticipation of favours in return. In this chapter we will examine the topography of cults and various rituals of Greek religious practice and then turn our attention to the vast array of deities and heroes that make up the pantheon of Greek religions.

Sanctuaries and religious architecture

Sanctuaries, ground sacred to one divinity or several, varied considerably in location, size and furnishings. They could be situated on an acropolis above the

84 Aerial view of the sanctuary of Apollo at Delphi. Situated on a terrace on a rising slope, the temple of Apollo with its famous oracle dominates the site. It is approached by a zigzag sacred way, which was lined with marble treasuries dedicated to the god by various city-states (the Athenian treasury is reconstructed at the lower left). Above the temple and carved into the hillside is the theatre where musical contests were held at the quadrennial festival of Apollo known as the Pythia.

city (as in Athens), within the urban setting, outside the city proper (known as extra-mural), and at the boundaries of the territory of a *polis*. The rural sanctuaries of Olympia, sacred primarily to Zeus, and of Delphi, home of the oracular Apollo, are two of the largest; they attracted Greeks from all over the Mediterranean, as well as foreigners, many of whom made lavish dedications. In addition to the temple or temples to the major deity, there were smaller shrines to other gods and goddesses, treasuries to house the dedications of individual city-states, dining rooms, athletic facilities, and in some cases a theatre for musical contests or theatrical performances. Outside the walled temenos were facilities for the festival participants, such as stadiums, gymnasiums, palaistras, hippodromes, and hotels.

The focal point of a sanctuary was, however, the altar and it alone could constitute the locus for religious activity. Altars may have been modest mud-brick structures initially but later stone ones could reach huge proportions, as for example the gigantic 198-metre-long altar built by Hieron II at Syracuse in the later third century. Sometimes they were lavishly decorated, as the Great Altar of Zeus at Pergamon (*c.* 165) which featured a 110-metre-long frieze around its podium depicting the battle of the gods and giants (see Chapter 9, fig. 170). The unusual ash altar of Zeus at Olympia consisted of the accumulated

The Parthenon

The immense rock known as the Acropolis dominates the heart of the ancient and modern city of Athens. At a height of 157 m above sea level and with nearly vertical slopes, except at the west, it constituted an impregnable citadel and an impressive stage for the worship of the city's patron goddess Athena. While other gods such as Zeus and Artemis had shrines here as well, the trio of marble temples constructed in the second half of the fifth century to honour Athena in her guises of Parthenos (Virgin, right rear), Polias (city patron, centre rear) and Nike (Victory, right front) are some of the most remarkable and beautiful monuments of the ancient world. The Temple of Athena Polias, also known as the Erechtheion, housed the old sacrosanct statue of the goddess made of olive wood. This three-roomed temple had an unusual plan and is best known for its 'Porch of the Maidens' which consisted of six caryatids in the place of columns, in the form of draped women with baskets on their heads. The tiny Temple of Athena Nike sat in its own precinct atop the projecting bastion created as part of the Bronze Age defences of the Acropolis. Both of these temples used the Ionic order with its volute-shaped capitals which was rare in mainland Greece. A fourth marble building known as the Propylaia (centre front) is equally impressive and served as a monumental entranceway to this imposing ensemble. It is in the Doric order on its two façades, has Ionic columns inside flanking the central passageway, and two projecting wings which serve to draw in the worshipper.

85 Acropolis reconstruction with Panathenaic procession.

86 Erechtheion caryatid, *c.* 420 BC.
H. 2.31 m. One of six *korai* or girls
supporting the small south porch
of the Erechtheion.

The Parthenon

87 Parthenon, 447–432 BC. Measuring 33.38 by 72.31 m, the Parthenon is the largest classical temple in mainland Greece and is constructed almost entirely of Pentelic marble, quarried a few kilometres from the Acropolis. Its architects were Iktinos and Kallikrates, who applied a proportional system of 4:9 throughout, so for example in the temple's width to its length, or the diameter of the columns to the distance between their centres. They also incorporated into the design all of the so-called 'refinements' of Greek temple architecture. Thus there are no horizontal or vertical lines; all elements are bowed, from the curvature of the foundations to the slight bulging of the columns. These small deviations result in a building that has a uniquely life-like quality.

88 Athena Parthenos, gold and ivory statue by Pheidias, *c.* 438 BC. Nashville Parthenon's recreation by Alan LeQuire, AD 1982–2002. One of the most spectacular monuments of antiquity once stood inside the cella of the Parthenon. Soaring to 12 m and covered with one metric ton of gold, this colossal Athena exemplified even more than the temple itself the pride, ambition and wealth of Classical Athens. From her triple-crowned helmet to the birth of Pandora on the base, this monument is replete with references to the powers of the city's patron deity. In the palm of her hand she literally holds victory (Nike), a clear allusion to the Athenians' role in defeating the Persians at Marathon in 490 and again at the battle of Salamis in 480.

89 'Strangford Shield', small-scale Roman copy of the shield of the Athena Parthenos by Pheidias. H. 42.5 cm. The exterior of the goddess' shield was decorated with a fierce battle between Greeks and Amazons on the slopes of the Acropolis. The two figures fighting side by side at the bottom are said to be concealed portraits of the sculptor Pheidias and the Athenian political leader Perikles.

The Parthenon

90 East and west pediments, engravings published in
1830 from drawings by the artist Jacques Carrey,
1676. The marble pedimental sculptures narrate two
important events in the life of the goddess Athena:
her birth (east) and her contest with Poseidon for the
hegemony of Athens (west). Over life-size and carved
entirely in the round, the gods and heroes of the
pediments present a brilliant solution to the problem
of fitting a unified narrative into a low triangular space
without sacrificing unity of scale. In the more violent
action portrayed on the west, Athena and Poseidon,
flanked by their chariots, move dramatically apart.
In the calmer east pediment, where Athena once
stood at the centre with her enthroned father Zeus,
the reverberations of her dramatic birth seem to
radiate out to the other deities standing, seated or
lying nearby. At the furthest corners the rising sun
god Helios and the descending moon goddess Selene
indicate both the location (heaven) and the time of
day (sunrise).

91 South metopes 2 (left) and 27 (right). The outer frieze of this Doric temple consists of triglyphs alternating with square plaques known as metopes, of which the Parthenon has ninety-two. All are sculpted with battles: that of the gods and giants on the east, and between heroes and foreigners (Trojans, Amazons, centaurs) on the other three sides. Best preserved are the south metopes, which depict the wedding of the hero Peirithoos to which the centaurs of nearby Mt Pelion were invited. Drunk on a surfeit of wine, they attacked the female guests and so the Lapith youths fought them in these varied two-figure compositions, just as they battle the Amazons on the less well-preserved west metopes. Both foes are 'barbarians' and so allude to the Persians, who had attacked Greece in the recent past. (For a coloured reconstruction of another south metope, see Chapter 7, fig. 137.)

The Parthenon

92 Below: Colour reconstruction of Parthenon frieze in situ.

The inner or Ionic frieze is the most anomalous feature of the Parthenon. It runs for 160 metres along the top of the temple walls and over its two porches, and depicts several hundred mortal Athenians in the Panathenaic procession. Many are mounted on elegantly prancing horses while others drive racing chariots; several direct traffic, and some carry sacrificial paraphernalia or lead animals – and most are handsome youths. However, the east side features women at the head of the procession, and at its very centre over the east doorway is the priestess of Athena. Along with the priest and three younger attendants, she is involved in the presentation of the robe (*peplos*) to the goddess Athena, who sits nearby with her fellow Olympians.

93 Top left: West frieze block II (cavalcade).
Top right: South frieze 44 (youths with cow).
Above: East frieze (*peplos* ceremony).

94 Frieze slab of the Temple of Apollo at Bassai, *c.* 400 BC. L. 1.25 m. The manner in which the Greek hero pushes his knee into the back of the centaur while pulling his hair is reminiscent of the second south metope of the Parthenon. It is recorded in ancient sources that Iktinos, who designed the Parthenon, was also the architect of this temple to Apollo in the central Peloponnese.

ashes, melted fat and burnt bone from centuries of sacrificing oxen and reached a height of over six metres, according to Pausanias. Altars were set up in many places besides sanctuaries, namely houses, theatres, *bouleuteria* or any other location where it was necessary to invoke the gods. In vase paintings altars are often depicted streaked with blood, indicating the frequency of animal sacrifice and thereby demonstrating the piety of the worshippers.

A temple or *naos* was built when the need arose to house a cult statue of the divinity. The Greek stone temple as we know it, with its rectangular ground plan surrounded by stately columns, has its origin in simple one-room shrines with porches in front to shed the rain. These were aggrandized by elongating the plan and surrounding them with wooden posts, as in the house/shrine at Lefkandi (Chapter 3, fig. 31). In the seventh century these structures were adapted from mud brick and wood into stone, and while the techniques of stone working, and perhaps even the form of the base-less fluted Doric column, were adapted from the Egyptians, many of the other singular elements, such as painted triglyphs, guttae and regulae, derive from some form of wooden prototype. While the Doric order prevailed in mainland Greece and the west, the Ionic with its volute capitals is found predominantly in the east, that is, western Turkey and the islands. The leafy Corinthian order, actually a variant of the Ionic since it had a similar base and fluting, developed in the late fifth century and became very popular with the Romans.

Given the conservatism of Greek religion, temple architecture appears to have changed little over the centuries. However, it did evolve subtly from the elongated seventh- and sixth-century temples, to a ratio of 4:9 in the mid-fifth-century Parthenon, and became gradually shorter in the subsequent centuries. The Doric column, whose height is directly proportional to its lower diameter, grew slimmer and its capital (*echinus*) developed a tauter profile. Most of the sculptural decoration of temples was on the exterior and this increased, culminating in the Parthenon with its ninety-two sculpted metopes (compared to twelve on the Temple of Zeus at Olympia, *c.* 470) and its anomalous Ionic frieze. A trend towards greater internal elaboration can be seen in the Temple of Apollo at Bassai with its interior frieze of Greeks fighting Amazons and Lapiths contending with centaurs, subjects which had earlier appeared on the exterior of the Parthenon. In the Hellenistic period some temples were given more dramatic settings, reached by flights of steps and surrounded by colonnaded stoas. Variations on the plan of the traditional rectangular temple include the circular tholos with its ring of columns surrounding a round building, as in the sanctuaries of Athena at Delphi or the healing god Asklepios at Epidauros. In the later fourth century monumental tombs of kings and Persian satraps took on the appearance of a colonnaded temple, namely the underground chamber tombs of the royalty of Macedonia, or, in south-eastern Turkey, the Nereid Monument and the Mausoleum at Halikarnassos (see Chapter 8, figs. 151 and 156).

Rituals

Occasions for religious rituals in ancient Greece were many, ranging from a simple celebration of the birth of a child around the family hearth to lavish week-long civic festivals with attendant contests, hecatombs or sacrifices of a hundred animals, and elaborate processions. Whether the ritual took place in a large sanctuary or at a small shrine, it was preceded by a procession to the god's altar. At major civic festivals, like the Panathenaia illustrated on the Parthenon frieze, a large number of citizens, women, metics and foreign dignitaries took

95 Votive relief dedicated to the Thracian goddess Bendis, *c.* 400–375 BC. H. 52 cm. Imported from the north of Greece (Thrace) in 432, the worship of the non-Olympian goddess Bendis involved a nocturnal torch race on horseback. Here we see the winning team in a procession towards the larger than human-size goddess.

96 Archenautes sacrificing at an altar. Athenian red-figure stamnos attributed to Polygnotos, *c.* 450 BC. H. 40 cm. The worshipper on this vase and his two young nude assistants are named, and the scene might represent an actual sacrifice taking place in Athens in the mid fifth century. However, the presence of the winged goddess Nike hovering over the altar with a libation jug adds an element of fantasy. The boys are roasting meat on spits to the tune of the aulos, while the choice portion which includes the tail is already curling up in the flames, an auspicious sign.

97 Man pouring a libation to Hermes onto a flaming altar. Athenian black-figure neck amphora, *c.* 500–480 BC. H. 27 cm. Here a man in festal attire is pouring wine from his jug on to a blood-streaked altar. He raises his left hand in a gesture of worship and gazes at a herm which represents the god Hermes. Herms were very common in Athens and the countryside and consisted of a pillar with a bearded head on top and male genitalia below.

part. The procession to Olympia from the town of Elis at the start of the Olympic Games covered 58 km and took two days. On the other hand, at small family rites the members of the *oikos* including children and servants proceeded on foot to the local shrine or altar.

The most sacred act of religious ritual was that of animal sacrifice, and the Greeks normally consumed red meat only on festival days. In an agrarian society the most generous offering was a domesticated animal. It could range in size from a large ox or cow to a goat, piglet or lamb, which were more common, depending on the occasion and the wealth of the worshipper. Birds were also sacrificed, as we know from Sokrates' last words, 'a cock for Asklepios'. The animal was lured with grain carried in a special basket known as a *kanoun* to the altar, where its throat was slit, a moment rarely shown in the over 400 vases depicting animal sacrifice. The entrails were immediately roasted for the priest and his attendants, the bones and fat burned for the gods, and the meat distributed to the participants for boiling in pots. Although the gods seem to have been short-changed, they were said to enjoy the aroma of the burning fat.

A simpler form of communication with the gods, and one they are often shown performing themselves, is the libation. Liquid is poured onto an altar for the Olympians, and on the ground for chthonic or underworld deities, such as Hades and Persephone, and immortalized heroes. Typical libation vessels are the oinochoe or wine jug, and the phiale or shallow bowl, often made of metal (see Chapter 7, fig. 133 and Chapter 8, fig. 145). Libations were offered to the gods at the beginning and end of most solemn occasions, such as a symposium, the opening of the Assembly, or the beginning of a trial.

Gifts for the gods were another important act of worship, mentioned as early as the *Iliad* where the Trojan queen Hekabe places a woven robe on the lap of the statue of the goddess Athena. When he won a bronze tripod at a musical contest the eighth-century Boiotian poet Hesiod dedicated it to the Muses. Even foreign kings, like the wealthy Kroisos of Lydia, made lavish offerings in Greek sanctuaries; he dedicated a gold lion weighing ten talents to the oracle at Delphi. Gifts could be made for blessings received (as in the case of Hesiod) or for favours sought, as in the case of Kroisos who desired a specific response from the oracle. Tithes or first fruits were commonly cited as the reason for the

98 Bronze statuette of a woman, *c.* 480 BC. Her dress is inscribed 'Aritomacha dedicated this to Eleuthia'. Eleuthia was the Greek goddess of childbirth to whom mothers-to-be would pray for a successful delivery.

99 Axe from Sant'Agata, Calabria, *c.* 500 BC. H. 16.5 cm. The blade is inscribed 'I am sacred to Hera in the Plain. Kyniskos the butcher dedicated me, a tithe from his work'.

100 Cult statue of Demeter from Knidos, *c.* 350 BC. H. 1.5 m. This life-size marble statue of an enthroned goddess was found at the site of Knidos in south-west Turkey, the sanctuary of Demeter, the goddess of fertility, and the underworld deities Hades and Persephone with whom Demeter was also worshipped. The preservation of cult statues is rare and this example is exceptionally well carved, with the face being of a finer marble than the body.

dedication on inscribed objects, and sick persons often dedicated a model of the particular body part that needed curing. In the fourth century statues of young children are frequently found in sanctuaries, no doubt thank offerings from grateful parents. Garments do not survive but they are listed in inventories as offerings (some even listed as 'rags') especially to the goddess Artemis after childbirth. Weapons are also common in shrines of Zeus, Athena and Apollo and were undoubtedly dedicated by the victors in thanks for their survival after battle.

Oracles and mysteries

The Greeks' obsessive desire for knowledge manifests itself in several religious rites which are characteristic of their beliefs. One is divination in the form of prophesies and oracular responses and another is initiation into mystery cults. The Greeks shared with many other ancient religions the arts of divination via observations of phenomena such as the flight of birds, the condition of an animal's liver, or the throw of dice-like objects known as knuckle-bones. Prophets and seers who interpreted dreams and other unusual events are mentioned in the Homeric epics and continued to play an important role in Greek religion. Mystic initiation, besides being a life-changing experience, carried a great deal of prestige and many undertook the lengthy and costly process.

Although Delphi is the best-known oracle, there were several other famous oracular shrines in the Greek world, such as that of Zeus at Dodona where the movement of the leaves in a tree, the 'talking oak', served as the oracular response. One unusual aspect of the oracle at Delphi is that the medium was a virgin girl, since male gods normally had male priests.

The rite of initiation into mystery cults still remains a well-guarded secret but we know that it became increasingly popular over time. This is demonstrated at Eleusis where every year the international festival in honour of Demeter and Persephone took place in an ever grander columned hall known as the Telesterion.

Gods

Like the gods of the ancient Near East and Egypt, the Greek gods were anthropomorphic as well as zoomorphic. The Olympians were represented in human form and although immortal nonetheless had many of the foibles of humans, the infidelities of Zeus being a classic example. They could assume animal forms, or that of a bird – as the owl for Athena, eagle for Zeus or goose of Aphrodite. Minor deities were often hybrids, like the rustic god Pan who had the horns, tail and legs of a goat. The Greeks believed that every manifestation of nature from rivers to constellations was semi-divine, and many natural phenomena were the result of divinely wrought metamorphosis; thus the youth Narcissus became a flower and the grieving Niobe was transformed into a rocky mountain.

The Greeks had a deity to pray to and propitiate for every important experience of human life. Hera, the wife of Zeus, oversaw marriage while Aphrodite's domain was erotic love. The huntress Artemis was prayed to during the pangs of childbirth, and her twin brother Apollo was a god of health and the father of Asklepios, the god of healing. Bloody warfare was the concern of Ares, and his half-brother Hermes was a god of travellers. He conducted the souls of the dead to the underworld where Hades reigned with his abducted bride Persephone. Other gods supervised the necessities of life. As goddess of agriculture Demeter was responsible for life-giving grain. The foreign god Dionysos brought with him the gift of wine. Both Hephaistos and Hestia were associated with fire; for him the forge, and for her the domestic hearth. The Greeks gods often had more than one area of authority. Zeus, for example, was a sky god and so controlled thunder, rain and lightening, but was also a god of social concerns, like oaths. Characterized by her wisdom and cunning, Athena was a goddess of both battle strategy and craftsmanship. Not surprisingly she was born from the head of Zeus. Traditionally worshipped as the god of the sea, Poseidon was also responsible for earth-quakes and horses. A number of deities

101 Aphrodite and Pan playing knuckle-bones. Engraved bronze mirror from Corinth, *c.* 350 BC. Diam. 18.5 cm. As the goddess of love, Aphrodite is an appropriate subject for the decoration of a mirror, and here she is shown surrounded by figures frequently associated with her: her son Eros behind her and a goose below the table. Caught in a casual moment, she is playing a game of knuckle-bones with the rustic god Pan. The artist has deliberately contrasted the voluptuous and beautiful body of the goddess with the squat, goat-like body of her partner.

102 Zeus giving birth to Athena. Athenian red-figure pelike, *c.* 460 BC. H. 40 cm. A diminutive Athena is shown popping out of the head of her father Zeus at the moment of her birth. An ancient hymn to Athena gives this account:

Wise Zeus himself bare her from his awful head, arrayed in warlike arms of flashing gold, and awe seized all the gods as they gazed. But Athena sprang quickly from the immortal head and stood before Zeus who holds the aegis, shaking a sharp spear: great Olympus began to reel horribly at the might of the bright-eyed goddess, and earth round about cried fearfully, and the sea was moved and tossed with dark waves, while foam burst forth suddenly: the bright Son of Hyperion stopped his swift-footed horses a long while, until the maiden Pallas Athena had stripped the heavenly armour from her immortal shoulders. And wise Zeus was glad.

103 Nike, goddess of victory, erecting a trophy. Chalcedony gem, *c.* 360 BC. L. 3.3 cm. Once mounted on a swivel as part of a signet ring, this carved gem would also have been a good luck token. It shows the winged goddess of Victory (Nike) erecting a trophy which consists of a tree trunk covered with the captured arms of the vanquished enemy: a helmet, corselet, sword, spear, two shields and a greave.

104 Above: Wedding of Thetis and Peleus. Athenian black-figure dinos (bowl) signed by Sophilos, *c.* 580 BC. H. 71 cm. A procession of divinities on foot and riding in chariots encircles the top zone of this mixing bowl for wine and water. They are en route to celebrate the nuptials of the future parents of the hero Achilles, his mother Thetis who sits inside the house at right and his father Peleus who is greeting the guests.

105 Above right: Eleusinian Triad. Athenian red-figure skyphos by Makron, *c.* 480 BC. H. 20 cm. Triptolemos, who will distribute the gift of grain to mankind, sits in his special winged vehicle and is flanked by Demeter, the goddess of agriculture, and her daughter Persephone, who hold stalks of wheat.

are what we would call personifications, the most popular of whom were Eros the youthful god of Love, Nike the winged goddess of Victory, and Hebe the goddess of Youth. Not all gods had such positive images, for the Greeks also personified Fear (Phobos) and Strife (Eris). The Greek landscape was inhabited with a variety of nature sprites: nymphs in trees and fresh water springs, Nereids in the sea, maenads and satyrs in the countryside, winds and stars in the sky.

Various narratives were fashioned to provide a life story for the gods, of which the earliest was Hesiod's *Theogony*. Like the book of *Genesis*, Hesiod recounts the generations and parentage of the Olympians and countless lesser divinities. Many deities experienced miraculous births like Athena who emerged fully armed from the head of her father Zeus, were child prodigies like baby Apollo who slew the dragon guarding Delphi, and as adults performed astounding tricks such as transforming humans into beasts, mating with animals to produce monsters, and conferring immortality on their favourite heroes. The Olympians often acted in concert as when they took on the giants in battle, or when they attended the wedding of the sea nymph Thetis with the hero Peleus, a union that produced the hero Achilles.

Heroes

Heroes were the offspring of the gods' sexual unions with mortals, and while they were mortal they often had super-human abilities. Herakles, for instance, was born as the result of Zeus' liason with the mortal Alkmene. His infidelity incurred the wrath of Hera who tried to do away with Herakles by sending snakes to his cradle to strangle him. Naturally the hero prevailed, as he did in all his subsequent labours, and he eventually earned immortality. Some heroes like Theseus reputedly had two fathers: the mortal king of Athens, Aigeus, and the

106 Herakles and the Stymphalian birds. Athenian black-figure amphora, *c.* 540 BC. H. 40.6 cm. Here Herakles, the Greek hero par excellence, demonstrates his ability to bag a large flock of man-killing birds, armed only with a slingshot. He wears his traditional costume, the impenetrable skin of the Nemean Lion, his first conquest.

107 Below: Apotheosis of Herakles. Athenian black-figure kylix (detail), *c.* 540 BC. Diam. 27 cm. Herakles' completion of twelve gruelling labours gained him immortality. He is shown here entering Olympos, dragged into the presence of Zeus by his patron goddess Athena.

108 Left: Perseus beheading Medusa. Athenian black-figure olpe by the Amasis Painter, *c.* 550 BC. H. 25 cm. The beheading of the Gorgon known as Medusa by the hero Perseus is a favourite theme of Archaic vase painters. Because this monster had the ability to turn humans to stone, the hero has to look away while he plunges his sword into her neck. Her monstrous appearance is enhanced by her frontal face, bared teeth and the snakes that encircle her waist and head. The god Hermes stands at the right.

109 Below: Youthful deeds of Theseus. Athenian red-figure kylix by the Kodros Painter, *c.* 440–430 BC. Diam. 33 cm. The most notable deed of Theseus, his slaying of the Cretan Minotaur, is depicted in the centre of this elaborate Athenian wine cup. Around the unusual border are shown six more deeds of the hero (clockwise from top): wrestling Kerkyon, hammering Prokrustes, toppling Skiron from his cliff, capturing the Marathonian bull, flinging Sinis to his death, and slaying the vicious sow of the old woman Krommyo.

111

110 Opposite: Marble head of Asklepios from Melos, *c.* 325–300 BC. H. 61 cm. The head once topped a colossal statue of the healing god. He is portrayed in the manner of most older Greek gods, as bearded and with thick, shaggy locks of hair. He once wore a golden wreath.

immortal god Poseidon. Heroes were worshipped like gods with their own shrines and offerings.

The narratives of heroes are as various as those of the gods. They consist of group expeditions, such as the Argonauts' voyage to the Black Sea to acquire a golden fleece, or solo feats, like Perseus' beheading of the gorgon named Medusa. Gods and goddesses, especially Athena who is the patroness of heroes, are often depicted assisting them in slaying monsters. In Archaic art the labours of Herakles are among the most popular subjects, and figure prominently on vases and architectural sculpture produced in Athens. When the democracy was founded *c.* 510, the Athenians wanted to aggrandize their local hero Theseus and so invented a series of youthful deeds to add to his previously limited repertoire. These new deeds were illustrated on a series of special red-figure cups as well as on the metopes of the Athenian Treasury at Delphi, erected after 490.

An important figure of Greek religion who exemplifies the blurred line between heroes and gods is Asklepios. In the *Iliad* he is called a hero and he received his training in medicine from the wise centaur Cheiron, who tutored many other heroes in this art. And like heroes he had a divine father, Apollo, who was worshipped from at least the Geometric period as the god of healing. In the Classical period Apollo ceded some of his authority in this area to his son, who reputedly became so skilled in the arts of healing that he could raise the dead. This miracle incurred the wrath of Zeus who immolated him with his thunderbolt. In spite of the fact that he was mortal, the Greeks worshipped Asklepios as if he were a god. His cult was established alongside that of Apollo at Epidauros *c.* 500 and quickly spread throughout the Greek world, with major healing centres at Hellenistic Pergamon and Kos.

Epidauros was his main Panhellenic sanctuary which housed a small but lavish temple, an *abaton* where pilgrims slept in hopes of a dream cure, and a curious round temple or tholos which may have been his tomb since it occurs only here. A festival in his honour known as the Asklepieia necessitated the building of a theatre for musical contests and a stadium for athletic competitions. Unlike the Olympian deities he was considered a gentle and beneficent god. These characteristics as well as the legendary success rate of his cures – testified to by the numerous inscriptions on the site – increased his popularity. One woman claimed to have been pregnant for five years and only succeeded in giving birth when she visited Asklepios' shrine. We now turn to other, more credible, wonders of the Greek world.

7

Wonders to Behold

111 Opposite: Panathenaic prize amphora, *c.* 560 BC. H. 60 cm. Known as the 'Burgon Amphora' because it was found by Thomas Burgon in 1813 in an ancient cemetery in Athens where it served as an ash urn, this large oil jar perhaps was awarded to a victorious equestrian in the games held in 562 or 558 BC. On this side the goddess Athena is shown striding to the left where one reads the prize inscription 'one of the prizes at Athens' (TONATHENTHENATHLON). The other side shows a man racing a two-horse cart.

Having examined the solemnity of Greek religion in the form of processions, offerings, prayers and animal sacrifice, it is now time to turn to events that delighted the eyes and ears of both gods and humans. Sporting contests, theatrical performances, music and choral dances, even acrobatics, were all part of Greek religious expression as were beautiful works of craftsmanship. Surprisingly the Greeks had no word for 'art', but referred to it as *techne* or craft. However, many of the terms for our cultural activities derive from Greek, indicating their origins in the ancient Greek world; for example, 'theatre' from *theatron* meaning a place for viewing, 'hippodrome' from *hippos* (horse) and *dromos* (track), and 'music' from *mousike* which refers to the art of the Muses, namely making pleasant sounds as well as poetry and dance.

These entertainments often took the form of competitions in which either individuals (athletes or poets), or teams (dancers or torch bearers) vied for a prize. In fact our term 'athletics' derives from the Greek word for 'prize' (*athlos*). Normally there was only a single prize for the first-place winner, but this did not discourage competition which was an integral part of ancient Greek life. Some of the prizes actually survive, like the amphorae once filled with olive oil that were awarded to athletes and equestrians at the Panathenaic games held in Athens. This pervasive spirit of rivalry no doubt stimulated athletes and performers to outdo one another and to push their skill to its peak. Winning often meant lasting acclaim or *kleos* for the victor, whether he was an Olympic athlete or a tragic playwright, in addition to more tangible rewards. Many of the victory odes commissioned from famous poets like Pindar and Bacchylides have survived, as have the bases of statues and monuments set up to honor victories in all sorts of contests from cavalry events to choral performances.

Ancient Greece is often said to be a performance culture, but a performance demands an audience. The Greeks devised and built special facilities to enhance performance and accommodate large audiences. Common to nearly every Greek city and major sanctuary in later times is the open-air theatre carved into a hillside and lined with semi-circular tiers of seats increasing in diameter as they rise up the slope, thus providing perfect viewing for the spectators. Roofed concert halls like the odeion built by Perikles in Athens served for musical performances, and stadiums were laid out with sloped sides for standing and

112 Theatre at Epidauros, *c.* 300 BC. This famous theatre at the sanctuary of Asklepios at Epidauros has legendary acoustics and provides stone seating for approximately 15,000 spectators.

113 Bronze statuette of a trumpeter from South Italy, *c.* 470 BC. H. 14.6 cm. A blast of the *salpinx* or trumpet announced the beginning of Greek games, and at Olympia there was a contest for trumpeters.

watching athletic contests. Before the advent of stone seating, open areas like the Agora were used for performances and the spectators were accommodated on temporary wooden seating.

Music and dance

Although not a single note of Classical music is preserved, it was omnipresent in ancient Greece. It accompanied weddings and funerals, sacrificial rites and dances, athletic training and military marches. Some of the earliest images in Greek art, Cycladic marble figurines and Bronze Age frescoes, represent musicians, and Homer's epics feature bards reciting their poems to the accompaniment of the lyre. Poetry and music were inextricably bound together, and distinctive types of song were deemed appropriate for specific occasions. The *paian* was sung in honour of Apollo, the *dithyramb* for Dionysos, the *threnos* at a funeral, and the *partheneion* for a dance of maidens. These melodies were called *nomoi* which literally means customs or laws, and so the term indicates the canonical and unvarying nature of these musical compositions, not unlike 'Happy Birthday' or national anthems. What little we know about Greek music indicates that it was fairly simple, with singer and instrument in unison, and no attempts at orchestral arrangements.

The two most common performance instruments were the lyre and the *aulos*, and within these categories of

114 Mousaios and two Muses. Athenian red-figure amphora attributed to the Peleus Painter, *c.* 430 BC. H. 57 cm. This scene displays four Greek musical instruments: the double pipes or *aulos* held by the standing Muse named Melousa, a cradle-*kithara* or *phormix* hanging in the background, an angle harp played by the seated Muse Terpsichore, and a tortoise-shell lyre held by the mythical Athenian musician and poet Mousaios.

stringed and wind instruments there were several variations. The *chelys* lyre, supposedly invented by Hermes, used a tortoise shell fitted with a leather hide as a sound box, while the more elaborate *kithara*, commonly held by Apollo and used by virtuosi performers, had a rectangular wooden sound box as seen on numerous vase paintings. The *aulos* (often mistranslated as 'flute') is akin to the modern oboe with its reed mouthpiece. What we call 'panpipes' is the ancient *syrinx* and it is often an attribute of the rustic god Pan. Finally the Greeks had a form of trumpet called a *salpinx* which was used by heralds before festivals and battle.

115 Above: Two *auloi* made of sycamore wood, 500–300 BC.

116 Left: *Aulos*-player and performer. Athenian red-figure amphora attributed to the Kleophrades Painter, *c.* 490 BC. H. 46 cm. One side of this vase shows a youth in festival dress playing the *aulos*; the leather strap across his face serves to keep his cheeks from bulging and to steady the instrument. On the other side is an older man reciting the first lines of a poem, 'Once upon a time in Tiryns …'. Both performers stand on low podiums, indicating that an aulodic contest is taking place.

One of the contests held on the first day of the ancient Olympics was that of the trumpeters, and the winner was given the privilege of signalling the start of the other competitions. While there were no other musical contests at Olympia, numerous festivals, like the Panathenaia (Athens) and the Pythia (Delphi), featured competitions in solo *kithara* and *aulos* playing, and in singing to the accompaniment of each. A more informal venue for music was the symposium, and vase paintings indicate that as the party and drinking progressed, the stately music of the lyre gave way to that of the rowdier *aulos*. In fact the most highly paid entertainer at the symposium was the 'flute-girl', and it was one of the first concerns of the Athens' police to control the prices offered for her services.

Music was a natural accompaniment to another art form that was both entertaining and competitive, namely dance. Dance in ancient Greece ran the gamut from the highly dignified to the outrageously obscene, and it was an activity in which both men and women took part, sometimes jointly. Contexts for dances range from the religious, in which choral performances were particularly prominent, to the symposium, at which young girls entertained the banqueters (see Chapter 4, fig. 63). There was also a great variety of dance competitions, such as the so-called pyrrhic which involved men dancing in armour.

117 Male and female dancers. Corinthian black-figure amphora (detail), *c.* 550 BC. H. 34.7 cm. These five so-called 'padded' male dancers are shown cavorting with three nude women, no doubt *hetairai*.

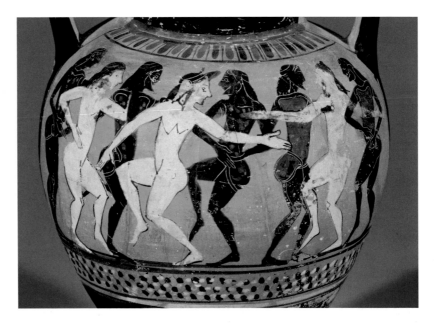

118 Dance lesson. Athenian red-figure hydria attributed to the Phiale Painter, *c.* 440 BC. H. 38 cm. A woman is teaching two young girls to dance while a potential customer looks on. A lyre hangs in the background.

119 Scene from Aischylos' *Eumenides* on a bell-krater from Paestum, *c.* 350–340 BC. H. 56 cm. Bloodied sword in hand, the matricide Orestes crouches as a suppliant at the shrine of the god Apollo. He looks up to his patron goddess Athena, while Apollo stares down at one of the two Furies tormenting the hero for the murder of his mother in the previous play of the trilogy, *Libation Bearers*. The tripod in the centre is a reference to the seat of the Delphic oracle.

Drama

Evidence suggests that the earliest rituals in honour of the god Dionysos took the form of masked choruses singing dithyrambs, which eventually developed into dramatic performances with the addition of the spoken word. Drama took three forms in ancient Athens where it seems to have begun at the City Dionysia festival held every spring: tragedy, satyr-play and comedy. Three tragedians were chosen to compete by writing three plays, each followed by the so-called satyr-play which provided comic relief. There were also three to five comedies presented, and so the Athenian audience saw fifteen to seventeen plays per festival spaced out over three to four days, sitting on their wooden, later stone, seats for up to ten hours a day. The chief archon of Athens chose the playwrights, the city paid the fees of the all-male actors, and a rich private citizen known as a *choregos* assumed the costs for the training and costuming of the chorus. Tragedies were usually based on myth in general and the epic tradition in particular, although plays dealing with contemporary events (Aischylos' *Persians*, in 472) are not unheard of. Comedies were contemporary fantasies and often parodies of tragedy. Only about one-tenth survives of the nearly 300 tragedies composed by the three most famous tragedians (Aischylos, Sophokles and Euripides), while eleven of Aristophanes' original forty comedies are extant.

These plays were performed first at the Theatre of Dionysos on the south slope of the Acropolis. We know little of ancient stagecraft other than what we can glean from the lines of the play, since there are no staging prompts. The tragic chorus consisted of twelve males (later fifteen), while that of comedy was twice as large. As for individual actors, the earliest tragedies had only one and he was the playwright. Aischylos was responsible for the introduction of a second actor, and his *Oresteia* of 458, the only extant trilogy, had three actors. Gradually the roles of the actors displaced that of the chorus in the development of the plot.

120 Scene from Euripides' satyr-play *Cyclops*. Lucanian calyx-krater of *c*. 415–410 BC. H. 47 cm. Above the drunken and sleeping Cyclops, Odysseus' companions are prying loose a tree truck to be used in blinding the monster. The two dancing satyrs at the right indicate that this scene derives from a satyr-play performed in honour of Dionysos.

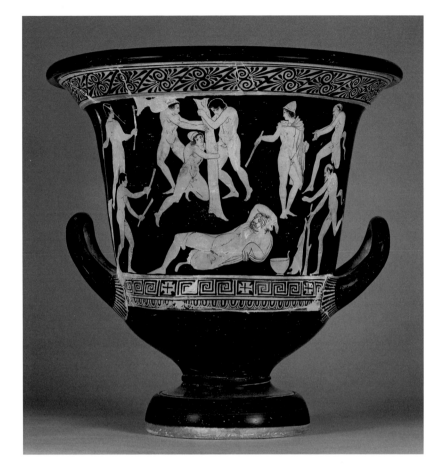

The chorus performed in the flat circle at the base of the seats known as the orchestra, while the actors entered and exited through a small building called a *skene*, which was probably painted to resemble a palace with doors. Theatrical apparatus consisted of a wheeled platform which could emerge from the doors, and a crane-like device known as the *mechane* for flying figures, such as Medea who escapes from Corinth in a snake-drawn chariot at the end of Euripides' play of that name.

Greek plays, and tragedy in particular, address many themes which still resonate with audiences today. Sophoclean tragedy explores the role of fate in men's lives in *Oidipous* who unwittingly murders his father and marries his mother and in the *Antigone* where the king, Kreon, denies a sister the right to bury her brother. Euripides in the *Bacchai* dramatizes the consequences of hubris or acting against the will of the gods in the downfall of the Theban king Pentheus who refuses to accept the god Dionysos, and in *The Trojan Women* exposes the frailty of the human condition in the fate of the Trojan queen Hekuba, reduced to slavery. Although many of the plays involve family murders

(*Agamemnon, Medea*) and suicide (*Ajax*), violence was never depicted on stage, although the corpse might be wheeled out after a murder. Comedies are less often reproduced today as much of the humour was topical, consisting of jabs at contemporary politicians *(Knights* in which Kleon is portrayed as an unscrupulous slave to Demos, the personification of the Athenian populace) or parodies of figures like Sokrates (*Clouds*). In Aristophanic comedy members of the chorus were often costumed to resemble creatures of nature (*Wasps, Frogs, Birds*), and the gluttonous hero Herakles was a stock caricature, sure to produce laughs.

121 Left: Marble portrait head of the Attic tragedian Sophokles from the Townley collection, Roman copy. H. 48.5 cm. At the age of sixteen Sophokles was chosen to lead the victory *paian* after the Battle of Salamis, and he was an actor in his youth. In addition to composing 120 plays (of which a mere seven survive), he was an Athenian treasurer and military general.

122 Comic actors (left to right): terracotta figurines of Herakles, a professional courtesan, and a slave taking refuge at an altar. H. *c.* 9 cm. The actors wore elaborate costumes and large masks, and so much of the acting consisted of gestures. The masks allowed actors to assume several roles and have large openings for the mouth in order to help project the spoken word.

123 Comic scene of the
centaur Cheiron. Apulian
bell-krater *c.* 380–370 BC.
H. 37.4 cm. Although there
is no surviving comedy
about the wise old centaur
Cheiron, this image with
its rustic stage and masked
comic actors with large
phalluses suggests there
may have been one.

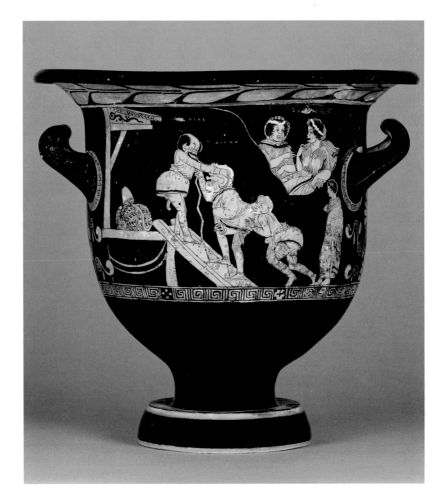

Athletic and equestrian contests

While Dionysos was honoured with theatrical contests, the feast days of other
deities were celebrated with athletic and equestrian contests. The oldest and
most prestigious of these festivals was that in honour of Zeus at Olympia in the
Peloponnese, traditionally dated to 776. The Olympics were held every four
years thereafter until AD 393 when the early Christian emperor Theodosius I
banned all pagan cults. This festival was so pre-eminent that it served as a
calendar for the Greeks, and the victor in the footrace gave his name to the four-
year period known as the Olympiad. Zeus was also honoured by games held
every two years at the site of Nemea as was Poseidon at nearby Isthmia. The
other important quadrennial festivals with athletic contests were those of Apollo
at Delphi (Pythia) and Athena at Athens (Panathenaia). These latter games were
founded some 200 years after the Olympics, in the sixth century BC, and by
Roman times there were hundreds of Greek festivals with athletic competitions.

124 Three long-distance runners. Panathenaic prize amphora with lid, dated by inscription to 333 BC. H. 67 cm. By the positions of these runners' arms, held close to the body, it is possible to determine the length of the race; it is not a sprint in which the arms are flung outwards, but rather the long-distance race.

125 Hoplitodromos or race in armour. Athenian red-figure cup, *c.* 480 BC. Diam. 30.5 cm. Two armed runners approach a judge after passing the turning post at the right. The winner is looking back at the runner-up, who has dropped his shield.

126 Boxers and wrestlers in the pankration with trainer. Athenian red-figure cup, *c.* 480 BC. Diam. 30.5 cm. The youthful but already disfigured boxers at the left are practising, while in the bout between the two pancratiasts at the right fouls are being committed in the form of eye gouging and possibly biting. The trainer is about to intercede with his forked stick.

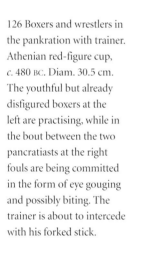

At the first Olympics the only event was the sprint from one end of a track to the other. Gradually longer distance races were added, and even a foot race in armour known as the *hoplitodromos*. The stadium was also used for the pentathlon which consisted of five events: running, discus, javelin, broad jump and finally wrestling. This competition involved a variety of equipment, some of which survives as dedications in sanctuaries or in tombs: javelins with a leather loop for the fingers; bronze discuses of various weights and sizes; and hand-held jumping weights of lead and stone. There is still much debate about the scoring

127 Four pentathletes: jumper, two javelin-throwers, and a discus-thrower. Panathenaic prize amphora, *c*. 525 BC. Because the pentathlon involved exercising both legs and arms, these athletes were considered to have the most handsome bodies.

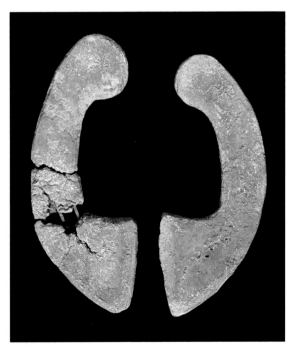

128 (left) Pair of lead jumping weights (W. 1.07 kg each) and (above) a bronze discus (W. 1.25 kg). This metal athletic equipment is depicted in white on the vase showing the pentathlon (fig. 127).

129 Bronze statuette of a female runner. Probably from Sparta, *c.* 500 BC. H. 4 cm. This small bronze of a girl athlete corresponds closely to the description provided by Pausanias of female runners at Olympia 'they bare the right shoulder as far as the breast'.

of this event, but we do know that if an athlete won three of the first four events he was spared the last, wrestling. Wrestling was also a contest in its own right, along with other combat sports like boxing and the pankration. In boxing the hands and wrists were wrapped in leather straps, but there was no head protection and one often encounters bloodied, disfigured faces of boxers in Greek art. Probably most violent of all was the pankration with few holds barred; only biting and gouging were prohibited.

Contestants were grouped by age and at Olympia there were contests for boys and men, while at the Panathenaia there were three age categories. The athletes competed in the nude, as we see on numerous vases depicting Greek athletics, and married women were not allowed to attend the games at Olympia on pain of death. However, there were competitions for girls held at another time in honour of Hera. The Heraia competition consisted of a short foot race in the stadium, and the winners were allowed to dedicate images of themselves in the Temple of Hera.

Then as now, the most prestigious events were those involving horses. Only the wealthy could compete and the owners rather than the jockeys received the prize. Thus a woman could enter a chariot team at Olympia and be hailed the winner, even if she were not there to witness the event – as

130 Winner in an equestrian contest. Athenian black-figure amphora, *c.* 520–500 BC. H. 45 cm. A victorious jockey is accompanied by his groom who carries the prize tripod and a wreath while a herald in front proclaims the name of the victor.

132 Right: Victory cere-
mony in the torch race at
Athens. Athenian red-
figure krater signed
by the potter Nikias,
c. 420–410 BC. H. 37.4 cm.
As the elderly priest at the
altar of Athena proclaims
the winner of the torch
race, a winged Nike flutters
in to tie a fillet on his body.
Inscribed on his headband
is the name of the victor's
tribe (Antiochis) which
is also the tribe of the
potter who signed on the
underside of the vase.

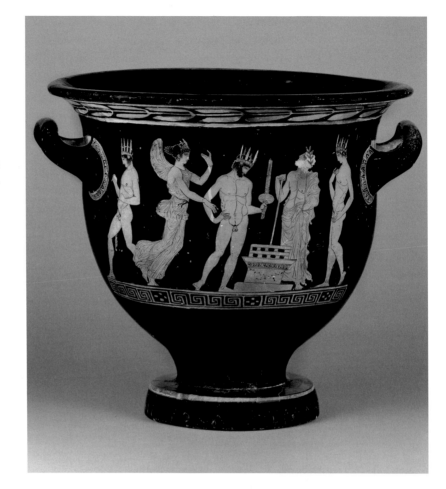

131 Opposite: Mounted
riders throwing javelins
at a target. Panathenaic
prize amphora, c. 390 BC.
H. 71.2 cm. The javelin
throw on horseback was
not an Olympic event, and
was probably introduced at
the Panathenaia in the mid
fifth century BC when the
Athenian cavalry was
expanded.

in the case of Kyniska, the sister of the king of Sparta who won twice and set up
a statue proclaiming her victories. There was a great variety of equestrian events
from a race for young colts to a quadriga race which included ten vehicles and a
total of forty horses racing around the hippodrome. At Athens a special age-old
contest known as the *apobates* involved a four-horse chariot with charioteer and
an armed warrior who jumped on and off until he dashed to the finish line. This
tribal race was run in the Agora and is magnificently represented on both the
north and south sides of the Parthenon frieze.

The Panathenaia in Athens was distinctive among Greek festivals in
sponsoring team events limited to its own citizens, who competed according to
their ten tribal units. These intramural contests included pyrrhic dancing for
three age categories; the torch relay race which conveyed fire from the Academy
to the Acropolis; a 'contest of ships', presumably a boat race at the port of
Piraeus; and a mysterious event known as *euandria* or 'manly excellence',
possibly a male beauty contest.

'Marvels'

When Homer used the expression '*thauma idesthai*' ('a wonder to behold') he was inevitably speaking of a work of exquisite craftsmanship – a beautifully wrought chariot, or a splendid shield with intricate narrative scenes. These *objets d'art*, usually manufactured from precious metals, are praised for their gleaming brightness. It is no surprise then that the now-lost chryselephantine cult statue of Zeus at Olympia by Pheidias was considered one of the seven wonders of the ancient world. Nor is it surprising that for the ancient Greeks bronze sculpture was more prized than even the finest Parian marble. Although Pheidias' statues have long since disappeared and most bronzes were melted down in antiquity and later, the effort lavished on vessels which chance to survive demonstrates the Greeks' love of gold and silver in finely crafted shapes and designs.

Artists, it seems, were no less competitive than athletes. A story is recorded of the commissioning of a wounded Amazon statue for the sanctuary of Artemis at Ephesos. Five of the most renowned sculptors, including Pheidias, competed and the winner was Polykleitos, because the other four artists all voted his statue second after their own. And even when artists were not officially competing, one

133 Silver phiale from Eze, France, *c.* 300 BC. Diam. 20.6 cm. This type of shallow bowl with a knob in the centre is known as a phiale, and was used for pouring libations to the gods. This silver example is elaborately decorated in concentric relief bands. The widest shows five racing chariots, driven by winged Nikai and carrying four divinities (Athena, Ares, Hermes and Dionysos) and the hero Herakles.

134 Gold glass bowl from Canosa, Italy, *c.* 270–200 BC. Diam. 20 cm. This 'sandwich glass' bowl which comes from a tomb in southern Italy is a technical masterpiece. It comprises two transparent glass bowls fused together after the gold leaf was applied to the exterior of the inner bowl. The filigree-like designs consist of elaborate florals and acanthus leaves.

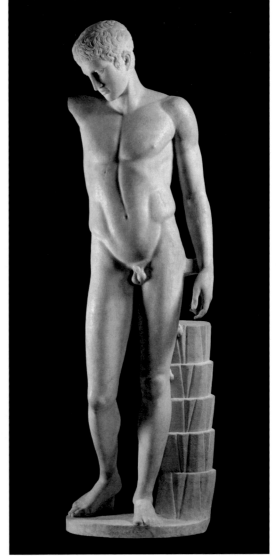

135 'Strangford Apollo' or marble kouros, *c.* 490 BC. H. 1 m. The strict frontality and symmetry of this male nude is characteristic of Archaic sculpture, which adopted the stance and proportions from Egypt. The divisions of the abdomen are linear and the coiffure consists of a row of stylized snail-shell curls. The kouros is a type of Archaic sculpture that both stood on a grave and was dedicated in a sanctuary.

136 'Westmacott Athlete', *c.* 440 BC. H. 1.5 m. Polykleitos, sculptor of this athlete, was renowned in antiquity for his representations of victors in athletic contests. His original, of which this is a Roman copy, was in bronze and may have represented a young boxer named Kyniskos, whose statue base still exists at Olympia. Polykleitos developed a formula for the perfect male figure which is reflected in this statue. The left leg bears the figure's weight and his right arm is raised, perhaps holding an olive-leaf crown, while the limbs on the opposite sides are relaxed. Compared to the late Archaic 'Strangford Apollo' (left), he exhibits more movement and naturalistic musculature.

Colour

Ancient written sources attest to the painting of marble sculpture in ancient Greece. The sculptor Praxiteles expressed a preference for those of his own works which the painter Nikias had coloured. Recent study of the surfaces of marble sculpture under special lighting conditions has revealed traces of previously undetected paint. While the extensive colour on this painted cast of a metope from the south side of the Parthenon may look garish to our eyes, unpainted marbles would no doubt have appeared strange to the ancient Greeks, who prized verisimilitude.

137 Painted reconstruction of a metope of a Lapith battling a centaur from the Parthenon.

can detect a competitive streak. On his amphora depicting men revelling in ambitious poses, an early red-figure vase painter added an inscription which claims that his rival never painted as well. In sculpture one can see how each successive generation of sculptors improved upon their predecessors' work, creating ever more naturalistic musculature, more realistic drapery, more animated poses and more life-like expressions. Likewise in the medium of ceramics, Athenian vase painters made a dramatic switch *c.* 530 from black-figure, which had been the norm for a century, to red-figure. The new technique allowed artists to paint rather than incise the inner details and thus make the figures more life-like than the previous black silhouettes. The greatest loss from antiquity is colour, since the monumental wall paintings that are described in ancient authors no longer survive and sculpture has mostly lost its once bright polychromy.

8

The Greeks Overseas

138 'Berber head'. Bronze portrait head from the Temple of Apollo at Cyrene, Libya. H. 30.5 cm. The Greeks' fascination with foreigners is exemplified by this unusually sensitive treatment of a man of African descent. Because the exact find spot is uncertain, its date is problematic and scholars have offered a range of possibilities between the fourth and second centuries BC. However, because it was found in a sanctuary of Apollo and the life-size statue was originally of bronze, it may represent a victorious athlete.

A stunning bronze portrait head that, at first glance, suggests a slightly hirsute Greek can, upon closer inspection, be identified as a man of North African descent. His full lips, once copper plated, high cheekbones and moustache are not 'ideal' traits in the Greek aesthetic, handsome though they are. This head, perhaps once part of a life-size equestrian statue, demonstrates the wide-ranging and profound impact of Greek culture throughout the Mediterranean, its appeal to foreign elites as well as its selective adaptation to non-Greek contexts. The fact that a Berber prince might have travelled to Greece to compete in their religious contests testifies not only to the reach of Hellenic values but also to the cosmopolitan nature of life in the heartland of ancient Hellas.

Encounters between Greeks and foreigners go back to at least the Early Bronze Age and intensified during the Minoan and Mycenaean periods when we find evidence of trade, if not of permanent settlements, throughout the Mediterranean. During the Iron Age and later, Greeks travelled to foreign lands in a variety of capacities: as marauding pirates, hired mercenaries, maritime traders, itinerant craftsmen, exiled politicians, peripatetic philosophers, and most importantly for the future of classical civilization, as permanent colonists. In addition to Greek exports, particularly the ubiquitous pottery, further information about the Greeks overseas comes from literature and history. In Book 14 of the *Odyssey*, for instance, Odysseus tells a fictive tale of himself as a Cretan pirate who raids the coast of Egypt seizing women and children as slaves, a story which must have sounded credible to its Iron Age listeners. The voyage of the *Argo*, as told in the third-century epic *Argonautika* by the Alexandrian poet Apollonios of Rhodes but based on much earlier legends, points to pillaging expeditions in the Black Sea region. Herodotos speaks of Corinthian sculptors migrating to Etruria in early

139 Doric Temple at Paestum in South Italy, *c.* 460 BC. Known as the Temple of Hera II, this limestone building bears a close resemblance in plan and elevation to the Temple of Zeus at Olympia, constructed after the Persian Wars. When the Greeks migrated overseas they maintained close contacts with their homeland and kept up with changing styles of art, architecture, drama and literature.

times, and in the fourth century, following the devastating Peloponnesian Wars, Athenian ceramicists moved much of their operation to the lucrative markets of southern Italy. Colonists were so numerous in this region that it became known as Magna Graecia or 'Great Greece'. Even the Greeks who did not venture abroad came into regular contact with foreign products. A fifth-century comic poet remarks on the array of goods found in the market place: silphion and hides from Cyrene, mackerel caught in the Hellespont, pigs and cheese from Syracuse, Egyptian linen sails and papyrus, frankincense from Syria, Libyan ivory, slaves from Phrygia, nuts grown in Paphlagonia, dates and flour from Phoenicia, and carpets and cushions woven in Carthage.

A paradigmatic figure for the Greeks' overseas adventures is their greatest hero Herakles, who travelled the known world and beyond. His encounters speak volumes about the Greeks' view of foreign lands and peoples. As their geographical horizons widened, they embellished his legend with encounters reflecting their perceptions of foreigners or what modern parlance terms 'the Other'. According to assorted myths, Herakles travelled south to Crete to capture the bull that raped Europa, north to Thrace to raid the man-eating horses of Diomedes, east to the distant land of the militant Amazons to retrieve the war-belt of their queen, and to Troy to sack it for the first time while en route to the Black Sea together with the Argonauts. He travelled west to rustle the cattle of triple-bodied Geryon somewhere in distant Spain, drove them back across southern France and down the Tyrrhenian coast of Italy (supposedly with a stopover at the future site of Rome), thence to Sicily and, via the Adriatic coast, eventually back to Greece. In North Africa he visited the Atlas Mountains in quest of golden fruit, wrestled to death the ogre giant Antaios in Libya (according to Pindar, to prevent him from a barbaric act – roofing the Temple of Poseidon with the skulls of his victims!), and came to blows in Egypt with King Busiris, who sacrificed all foreigners but was unsuccessful in the case of almighty Herakles. He was once sold into slavery to a foreign queen (Omphale) and sired various sons with foreign women, such as Telephos, the son of Auge. Cattle rustling, horse thieving, the search for precious metals and slave trading were undoubtedly part of the common piracy that took place around the shores of the Mediterranean from Spain to the Black Sea. The uncouth behaviour of these exotic peoples at the fringes of the Greek world, however, was certainly exaggerated, although Herodotos does mention human sacrifice on the part of Skythians, Taurians and Thracians.

This chapter examines not only the impact of the Greeks on the areas they visited and colonized, but also what they learned and borrowed from other civilizations throughout the Mediterranean. The influence was hardly one way; seventh-century Greek art, for instance, is often called 'orientalizing' because of its undeniable debt to the art of the ancient Near East. In many instances Greeks intermarried with the native peoples in whose territories they settled and adopted some of their social, religious and funerary customs. Non-Greeks, or *barbaroi* as they were called since they did not speak Greek, in turn adopted Greek customs such as the symposium, the minting of silver coins, hoplite warfare and mythological narratives.

South: Egypt and North Africa

If the second book of Herodotos' *Histories* is any indication, Egypt was a source of endless fascination to the Greeks. Ionians of Asia Minor seem to have first come as mercenaries – the best evidence for which is the graffiti they incised on the colossal rock-cut statues of Rameses at Abu Simbel in the Upper Nile valley datable to the expedition of Pharaoh Psammetichos in 591 BC. His predecessor Necho presumably used Greek mercenaries in his campaign against Babylon in 605 BC, for the ruins of Carchemish on the upper Euphrates River produced Greek bronze weaponry, a greave and a large shield. In the later seventh century Greeks also sailed to Egypt but this time as traders. However, because Egypt limited access to foreigners, they were restricted to their emporia or trading posts in the Nile Delta, the best known of which is Naukratis, and never lived among Egyptians until Hellenistic times. Herodotos remarks on the xenophobia

140 Chiot bowl from Naukratis, *c.* 600 BC. Diam. 38 cm. As indicated by the incised inscription along the rim, this bowl was dedicated by a Greek man named Sostratos to Aphrodite and was found in her sanctuary at the trading colony of Naukratis, in the Delta region of Egypt.

141 Sherd of an Archaic East Greek amphora found at Naukratis. H. 7 cm. The earliest extant image of a black African in Western art appears on a mid-second millennium BC fresco fragment from Thera, and these exotic foreigners continued to exert a fascination for Greeks in all periods.

142 Head of Zeus Ammon on a silver tetradrachm of Cyrene, *c.* 480–470 BC. W. 12.87 g. At the Greek colony of Cyrene in North Africa Zeus was worshipped in the guise of Zeus-Ammon, hence the ram's horns, in deference to the famous oracle of the ram-god Ammon at Siwa in the Libyan desert.

137

143 Archaic kouros or youth (alabaster statuette from Naukratis, *c.* 550 BC, H. 10.2 cm), compared to an Egyptian striding figure of a king in grey granite (Ptolemaic, H. 91.5 cm). When the Greeks began to sculpt stone on a large scale their inspiration was the colossal stone statuary of Egypt. Close similarities can be seen in the stances and proportions of these male figures. The kouros, however, is nude, which was the norm for male figures in Greece.

of the Egyptians, claiming that 'No Egyptian, man or woman, will kiss a Greek, or use a Greek knife, spit, or cauldron, or even eat the flesh of a bull known to be clean, if it has been cut with a Greek knife.'

Naukratis was a composite community consisting of traders harking from cities in Asia Minor, whose presence is recognizable in part from their pottery, as well as Aiginetans, famed in antiquity as traders. Herodotos tells us that they individually founded sanctuaries for their favoured deities – so the Samians established a Heraion, and the Milesians one for Apollo – but the largest of all was a common sanctuary called the Hellenion, constructed by a league of Ionians, Dorians and Aiolians. Grain was the chief attraction for the Greek merchants who in trade brought wine and olive oil. Other commodities produced in Egypt that became regular imports to Greece in Classical times are linen and papyrus (although the Greek word for papyrus, *byblos,* suggests that it was first brought to Greece by way of the Phoenicians). Because numerous hoards with silver coins minted in Greece have been found in Egypt it is thought that these products were not only bartered but paid for with bullion, not otherwise available.

144 Ethiopian warrior. Athenian white-ground alabastron from Tanagra, *c.* 480 BC. H. 16 cm. This clay perfume vessel mimics its Egyptian alabaster model in shape and colour. The black-skinned archer with African facial features may be an Ethiopian at Troy or, if female, a Libyan Amazon.

While the Greeks in Egypt settled temporarily as traders, those in Cyrenaica (Libya) were farmers, attracted by the fertile soil and good rainfall. They originally emigrated from the Cycladic island of Thera *c.* 630 BC because of a severe drought, and were later joined by Dorian colonists from the Peloponnese and islands. In the sixth century Doric temples were erected for Apollo and Zeus, and a sanctuary of Demeter was established outside the city. The coins of Cyrene show how Zeus was syncretized by the addition of ram's horns with the god Ammon who had an important oracular shrine at the oasis of Siwa in the desert to the east. The reverse of the Cyrenaean coins highlights the rare plant silphion which grew only in this region and was highly valued for its medicinal sap.

The most momentous outcome of the Greeks' encounter with the ancient culture of Egypt was the adoption in the later seventh century of monumental stone architecture and sculpture. The art of quarrying large blocks of hard stone, the tools used to work and join them (hammer, chisels, clamps), and systems of proportions were lessons learned in Egypt and then adapted to different materials (limestone and marble) and uses. It is perhaps surprising that the Greeks did not attempt to copy the massive pyramids and needle-like obelisks so typical of Egyptian architecture (and which had an appeal to the Romans) but rather were impressed with smaller elements such as fluted columns and mouldings. The most striking similarities occur in sculpture, especially in the Archaic standing male figure, known as the *kouros* in Greek, which closely resembles Egyptian statues of similarly posed kings and officials. Computer analyses of the earliest Greek *kouroi* (pl. of *kouros*), many of which were colossal in scale, demonstrate that the Greek sculptors used the Egyptian system of applying a grid to all four sides of the block and mapping on to it the front, back and two profile views of the striding male with left leg forward, resulting in a four-square appearance to these first specimens of marble sculpture. Just as important are the changes from the Egyptian model which illustrate the different objectives of the Greek audience, namely nudity, absence of a back slab, and the Nemes headdress replaced by long patterned locks. While the rigid Egyptian statue was intended to last for eternity, the Greek counterpart was meant to be as life-like as possible to show itself capable of movement.

The Greeks borrowed minor art forms as well. One is the perfume flask known as an alabastron after its original Egyptian material. Greek ceramicists recreated its long tubular form in clay and often applied a white slip mimicking the original material. Intriguingly the shape seems to have been introduced to the Athenian Kerameikos by a sixth-century artist with a prominent Egyptian name, Amasis, who may have been a metic or foreign resident, as were many of the craftsmen in ancient Greece. Another import in the Archaic period was the nude female figure as a bronze mirror support. This non-Greek idea was short-lived and only appealed to the Spartans who had a tradition of female nudity and athleticism. The Egyptians in turn adopted little from the Greeks, perhaps because contact was so restricted, and it is not until Hellenistic times with the imposition of Macedonian rulers, that Egyptian culture becomes partially Hellenized.

West: Sicily, South Italy and Etruria

If the Greeks were constrained in their incursions into Egypt, they had the opposite experience in their movements west, resulting in some of the largest and richest city-states in the Greek world. Well before the Ionians managed a foothold in Egypt, Euboians from Chalkis had colonized the coasts of southern Italy and Sicily and were actively trading with the Etruscans of central Italy in metals. In fact the earliest Greek emporion or trading post in Italy, Pithekoussai (Ischia), is also the farthest north. Dates for the more permanent colonies

145 Gold libation bowl with six bulls. Probably western Greek, *c.* 600 BC. Diam. 14.6 cm. This phiale or libation bowl well illustrates the cultural mix characteristic of Archaic Sicily. It was found in a native Sikel tomb and is of Greek manufacture, but its decoration of a file of angular bovines is strongly influenced by Phoenician art. Archaeologists have concluded that it was probably made by a western Greek and presented to a Sikel king to secure a friendly alliance.

(*apoikia* or 'home away from home') are provided by Thucydides who states that the first (734 BC) in Sicily was at a site called Naxos in the shadow of Mt Etna, the largest volcano in Europe (3330 m). It was a natural, and easily sighted, landing spot for Euboian and Naxian sailors coming from the east and rounding the 'toe' of Italy, but not a very well protected harbour. The very next year Corinthian colonists located the most advantageous port on the east coast and founded what would become the major Greek city in the west, Syracuse.

Syracuse's colonial history is fairly typical of Greek colonies throughout the western Mediterranean. Settlers usually chose a well-protected site, either an off-shore islet (like Ischia) before settling on the mainland, or a small peninsula (like that of Ortygia, 'the quail', at Syracuse) before expanding inland to take advantage of the rich agricultural lands which supported the growing community. An accessible source of fresh water was also essential, and at Syracuse it was the famous Arethusa spring, the personification of which was

146 Etruscan bronze helmet from Olympia, *c.* 500 BC. H. 20 cm. Captured from the Etruscans by the western Greeks in their successful naval battle off Cumae in 474 BC, this helmet was then inscribed by the king of Syracuse Hieron I as a dedication to Zeus at Olympia.

featured on its coinage (see Chapter 4, fig. 46). These *apoikiai* quickly founded satellite cities to secure their boundaries; they were naturally farther to the west, as Syracuse's foundation of Kamarina or Megara Hyblaia's founding of Selinous on the south coast of the island. Because of the necessity of granting land equally to the individual settlers, a grid plan usually formed the layout of these colonies, and from their inception ample land was provided for the sanctuaries of the gods. In the sixth and early fifth centuries the western Greeks undertook ambitious temple construction projects, often vying with each other. Thus when Selinous built a temple to Apollo in the late sixth century that measured an enormous 50 by 110 m, the Geloan colony of Akragas topped it with one to Olympian Zeus just 3 m wider.

Life in these *nouveaux riches* colonies in the west was not entirely without problems. The Greek settlers often displaced the native populations who were pushed progressively inland. In general the colonists got along with the native Sikels, but occasionally there were confrontations as when the Sikel leader Duketios led a rebellion in the mid-fifth century BC. However, their major rivals were the Phoenicians from Carthage who established trading posts in western Sicily, Sardinia and Spain. In 480, supposedly on the same day that the mainland Greeks repulsed the Persians at Salamis, Geloan, the tyrant of Syracuse, routed Hamilcar's Carthaginian army at Himera on the north coast of Sicily. But at the end of the fifth century the tables were turned, and the westernmost Greek cities of Selinous and Akragas (Agrigento) were sacked by the Phoenicians and some of the loot made its way to the west of the island, as for example the recently discovered Parian marble statue of a Greek charioteer (see Chapter 1, fig.11).

Marble was not quarried in Italy until Roman times, so sculpture was generally carved from local limestone or fabricated in clay and fired. The western Greeks, like their Etruscan neighbours to the north, were skilled modellers in clay and the roofs of their temples were gaily decked out with colourful terracotta tiles and revetments. A speciality of this area, not produced in mainland Greece, was the portable terracotta altar with relief decoration, often decorated with mythological figures. In 443 BC the Athenians sent their

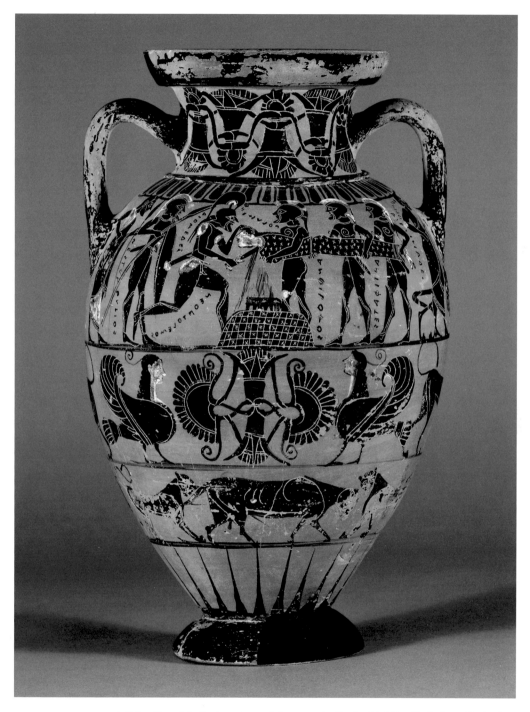

147 Sacrifice of the Trojan princess Polyxena at the Tomb of Achilles. Black-figure Tyrrhenian amphora produced in Athens, *c.* 570–550 BC. H. 37.5 cm. This type of vase was made specifically for export to Etruria, and its scene of female sacrifice was calculated to appeal to the tastes of the Etruscans, for this story is rarely depicted in Greek art.

148 Persian riding a camel. Athenian red-figure squat lekythos, late fifth century BC. H. 23 cm. The Athenians probably first encountered camels when the Persians used them in their invasion of mainland Greece in the early fifth century. This exotic beast of burden is shown in what looks like a Dionysiac procession with dancing women, but the male figures are wearing typical Persian dress.

first and only colonists to Italy where they founded Thourioi on the ruins of the famously luxurious city of Sybaris, destroyed by its neighbour Kroton seventy years earlier. One result of this new colony was the establishment of a flourishing ceramics industry; while the late fifth-century vases closely resemble Attic, in the next century the painters and potters expanded their repertoire, producing elaborate funerary kraters with multi-figured scenes, many derived from Greek drama (see Chapter 7, figs. 119–20).

Farther along in their voyages westward the Greeks collaborated with indigenous peoples to establish emporia for the importation of Greek luxury goods such as Attic black- and red-figured pottery, Chian wine and Laconian bronzes. The port towns of Graviscae and Pyrgi on the Tyrrhenian coast and Spina and Adria on the Adriatic served as entry points for these goods which were then distributed to the inland Etruscan cities. Happily for archaeologists, shiploads of these symposium vessels were deposited in the chamber tombs of the elite Etruscans and so survived to stock the museums of Europe. The most adventuresome Greek traders were the inhabitants of the East Greek city of Phokaia who were displaced when the Persians destroyed their *polis* in 540 BC. The Phokaian diaspora resulted in the foundation of Massalia (Marseilles) on the Rhône delta in southern France and Emporion in north-east Spain. These Greeks first brought the vine and olive to this region, and soon thereafter Massalia was exporting its own wine (ancestor of Burgundy) throughout the Mediterranean as evidenced by its distinctive transport amphorae recovered from ancient shipwrecks.

East: the Persian empire, Lycia and Karia

Contacts between Greeks and Persians existed long before their fateful encounters on the Greek mainland in 490 and 480/79 BC. All of Anatolia had been part of the Persian empire since at least the mid-sixth century when the Persians conquered the rich king of Lydia, Kroisos, in 546, and the western littoral of modern-day Turkey was ruled by satraps, or regional governors, responsible to the Persian

149 So-called Harpy Tomb, Lycia, south-west Turkey, *c.* 485–480 BC. H. 9 m. Drawing by George Scharf. While this pillar monument looks nothing like a Greek tomb, its sculpted reliefs were executed in the best Archaic style. It is thought to be the tomb of Kybernis, the ruler of the Lycian capital of Xanthos and the leader of the contingent of some fifty Lycian ships conscripted by Xerxes for his invasion of Greece.

150 Silenos led before the Phrygian king Midas. Athenian red-figure stamnos, *c.* 440 BC. H. 37.6 cm. The enthroned Midas' name is inscribed but he is readily identifiable by his ass's ears. The feathered fan held by the woman behind him is specifically mentioned by Euripides as a high-status attribute of wealthy Phrygians.

Nereid Monument

151 So-called Nereid Monument, partially reconstructed in the British Museum. From Lycia, south-west Turkey, *c.* 390–380 BC. H. 15 m.

Named after the life-size female figures with windswept drapery riding marine creatures set between its Ionic columns, this temple-like monument is actually the tomb of the Lycian dynast Erbinna. In its architecture it resembles the little Ionic temple of Athena Nike on the Athenian Acropolis, but the scenes carved in relief feature a non-Greek dynast in various Persian guises: conquering cities, hunting, feasting and enthroned under the shade of a parasol (as on the podium frieze illustrated here).

king. As the armies marched towards Greece many regions 'medized' or went over to the Persian side and produced contingents for the invading army and navy. One person offering valuable information to the Persians was the exiled Athenian tyrant Hippias, whose defection to the East was followed by that of other famous Athenian statesmen including Themistokles and Alkibiades. Although Persians were not successful in conquering Greeks on the battlefield, their luxurious life-style did have an impact. Attic vase paintings demonstrate that it became fashionable to sport Persian clothing, like the mitra or turban, and drink wine from metal animal-headed rhyta in the Eastern fashion. The practice of reclining at the symposium was also originally an Eastern custom, adopted by the Greeks along with the attendant furniture, elaborate wooden couches with ivory inlays, in the sixth century.

While the military invasions of Greece by Persia in the early fifth century are well known because they were recorded by Herodotos, the encounters of the Greeks with the Persians in their vast kingdom are less often mentioned. Xenophon's *Anabasis* is an account of 10,000 Greek mercenaries fighting on behalf of the Persian king Cyrus II who attempted to take over his brother's throne but was defeated in 401 BC. We have already noted how the Persians adopted the Athenian monetary standard and the imagery of the owl for their coinage. Greek sculptors left signs of their work at Persepolis, the Persian capital, and Greek emissaries bearing textiles are depicted in the reliefs.

Except for the Greek colonized littoral of western Turkey, the rest of Anatolia, or the modern country of Turkey, was part of the Persian empire from 546 BC until the arrival of Alexander the Great in 334 BC. The impact of Greek culture is particularly evident in the region of Lycia, in the south-west, which was ruled by dynasts from the capital of Xanthos. The Lycians, like the Etruscans, used the Greek alphabet to record their language and minted silver coins with images of Greek gods and heroes. Their distinctive pillar tombs are purely Lycian, but the reliefs decorating them were almost certainly executed by Ionian artists. The misnamed Harpy Tomb shows Greek sirens carrying off the souls of the deceased, and the women in their elaborate drapery resemble late Archaic *korai*. This pastiche of local tomb architecture with Greek funerary imagery demonstrates the aristocracy's taste for Greek elegance and sophistication.

Phrygia, like Skythia and Thrace, was a major source of slaves; according to epigraphical evidence about thirty per cent of the slaves in Athens originated in this region of north-central Turkey. Although Phrygians were regularly caricatured in Attic drama as cowards, they are not depicted thus in Attic vase painting. In spite of his donkey's ears, the legendary king Midas is always dignified. His historical namesake who ruled in the late eighth century was the first barbarian ruler to make lavish offerings to Apollo at Delphi.

152 Thracian woman pursuing Orpheus. Athenian red-figure amphora (detail), *c.* 470 BC. H. 32.5 cm. The 'barbarity' of the Thracians is exemplified by wild women with tattooed arms who attack the 'civilized' Greek musician Orpheus.

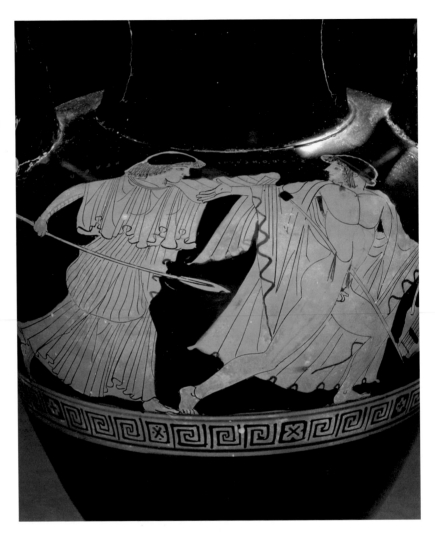

North: Thrace, the Black Sea and Skythia

Greek colonization to the north had a strong economic motive; these lands were rich in gold, timber, furs, fish and grain. The region of the Black Sea was one of the last major areas colonized by the Greeks and their settlements there were never truly independent. Hemmed in as they were by the Thracian tribes to the west and the Skythian nomads to the north, their colonies were precarious and depended on maintaining good terms with the locals to an extent not encountered elsewhere in the Greek diaspora. Athens, in particular, is noted for its links to the north as it relied heavily on imported grain to feed its population. Many of its famous leaders had connections here: the sixth-century tyrant Peisistratos owned mines in Thrace, and Perikles made a naval foray around

153 Thracian nurse. Fragment of an Apulian vase, *c.* 420 BC. H. 11 cm. Her tattooed arm identifies this female as a Thracian. She holds up her loosened garment with her teeth as she suckles an infant at her exposed left breast.

154 Skythian archer. Athenian black-figure plate, *c.* 510 BC. Diam. 19.3 cm. The exotic dress of this archer who is blowing a trumpet identifies him as a Skythian. It consists of a pyjama-like body suit, a pointed leather cap and a large bowcase at his waist. Noted archers, the Skythians introduced the socketed arrowhead to the Greeks and served as mercenaries in Athens in the second half of the sixth century BC when this plate was decorated.

155 Opposite: Peleus and
Thetis. Athenian red-figure
pelike by the Marsyas
Painter, *c.* 350 BC. H. 42.5
cm. These so-called 'Kerch'
vases were first found in
tombs at Pantikapaion
in the Crimea. They use
added colour liberally, as
in the blue wings of Eros
and the sea-green cloak
of the Nereid Thetis.

the shores of the Black Sea. Thracian women seem to have made a strong
impression on the Athenians for they were considered the best nursemaids for
their children, but ironically were also depicted attacking the musician Orpheus
in Attic vase paintings. In the fifth century Thracian dress became fashionable
for members of the Athenian cavalry who sported fox-skin caps (which can be
seen on the Parthenon frieze) and long thick patterned cloaks.

The Mausoleum

Perhaps the single monument that best exemplifies the commingling of Greek
and foreign cultures is the monumental tomb constructed for the Persian satrap
Mausolos in his capital city of Halikarnassos, in the satrapy of Karia on the west
coast of Anatolia. One of the seven wonders of the ancient world, this tomb
gives its name to all mausoleums. Little survives except parts of its marble
embellishment – sculptures in the round on various scales from the colossal to
life-size, and long narrative friezes. However, ancient descriptions give some
account of its size (134 m perimeter and 43 m tall) and its form: a tall podium,
surmounted by a peristyle of thirty-six Ionic columns, and a pyramidal roof.
Reconstructions vary but in essence the building incorporates a temple-like
colonnade with an Egyptian funerary monument, resulting in a unique
structure that resonates both in the East and West.

156 Reconstruction
of the Mausoleum of
Halikarnassos, *c.* 350 BC.

CHAPTER EIGHT

157 So-called statues of
Mausolos (H. 3 m) and his
wife Artemisia (H. 2.67 m).
These colossal figures
probably once stood
between the Ionic columns.

Pliny tells us that the most famous sculptors of Greece at the time were hired to carve the decoration: Skopas, Bryaxis, Timotheos and Leochares. The marble four-horse chariot on the summit was made by the architect Pytheos who, together with Satyros, wrote a lost treatise about the Mausoleum. In addition to the fragments of colossal figures, three frieze compositions survive: an Amazonomachy, a centauromachy and a chariot race. The first two recall earlier temple decoration like that of the Parthenon, while the chariots could represent the funeral games that Mausolos' wife and sister Artemisia may have held in his honour. This eclectic monument, which represents a meeting of the East and the West, brings us to the brink of a new phase of Greek history, the subject of the next chapter.

158 Frieze slab from the Mausoleum showing Greeks battling Amazons. H. 90 cm, This frieze was originally located at the top of the podium.

9

The Hellenistic World

159 Marble portrait of Alexander the Great, allegedly from Alexandria, Egypt, second–first centuries BC. H. 37 cm. Likenesses of Alexander were produced long after his death in 323 BC and became increasingly idealized. The dramatic turn of the head, the long luxurious locks and the slightly parted sensuous lips suggest a deified cult image rather than a realistic portrait.

A monument that could be said to epitomize the new world order created by Alexander the Great and carried on by his successors is the famous Rosetta Stone. A large slab of grey Aswan granite inscribed in two versions of Egyptian and in Greek, it is best known as the key to the decipherment of hieroglyphics. However, the Rosetta Stone also demonstrates how aspects of Hellenism were mapped on to local customs in what had been foreign – that is, non-Greek – territory, and not always without friction. The text alludes to a rebellion in the first year of the reign of the young Hellenistic king Ptolemy V on the part of Egyptians living in a town called Lykopolis in the Nile delta. The Egyptians were now subject peoples and politically, culturally and linguistically isolated from their Greek rulers, hence their occasional uprisings. While Egyptian priests still employed the old hieroglyphics and the common people used a newer 'demotic' version of the language, the third script expresses the linguistic *koine* that existed in Hellenistic times whereby Greek in a modified form of the Attic dialect became the official language. Most importantly, the text reveals how the institution of Macedonian kingship had been grafted on to that of the millennia-old Egyptian pharaoh. The young Ptolemy is addressed as 'great king of the upper and lower lands, son of the gods'. This notion of divine kingship was probably assimilated by Alexander during his brief sojourn in Egypt and magnified during his long march across Persia to India, in spite of objections from his Macedonian comrades in arms. It manifested itself in new modes of homage towards the king (*proskynesis* or ritual prostration), resented by his fellow Greek commanders as a sign of Persian arrogance, as well as of portraiture and imperial regalia.

160 Rosetta Stone. Fragment of a black granite stele found in 1799 near the mouth of the Nile at a site called el-Rashid (Rosetta). H. 1.14 m. This inscribed slab preserves three zones of script: Middle Egyptian hieroglyphic, Demotic or vernacular late Egyptian, and Greek. It records a trilingual decree passed by a council of priests on 27 March 196 BC, affirming the royal cult of the thirteen-year-old Ptolemy V on the first anniversary of his coronation.

As the Rosetta Stone indicates, Hellenism was a two-way street. Following the example of Alexander, the Macedonians adopted the customs, manners, art forms and even dress of their new subjects, while also bringing many features of Greek civilization such as coinage, city-planning, military science and classical ornament to the conquered peoples of the East. The spread of Greek culture was hardly a new phenomenon with the advent of Alexander but his conquests and policies helped to establish this wide-ranging and long-lasting cultural *koine*. During his inexorable march from Macedonia in northern Greece to the Indus

161 Silver tetradrachm minted by Lysimachos of Thrace, *c.* 283 BC. W. 7.25 g. Alexander the Great is shown with the diadem and ram's horn of the composite deity Zeus-Ammon (see Chapter 8, fig. 142).

162 Gold funerary wreath consisting of paper-thin oak leaves, acorns, two cicadas and a bee. Said to be from a tomb in the Dardanelles, *c.* 350–300 BC. Diam. 23 cm. Gold wreaths of oak, laurel, ivy, myrtle and olive have been found in burials from the fourth century onwards, and are associated with specific deities (Zeus, Apollo, Aphrodite and Athena). The most spectacular gold oak wreath was found with the cremated bones of a Macedonian king in the gold larnax discovered within the underground chamber tomb at Vergina.

River, a route of thousands of kilometres, this brilliant strategist not only conquered age-old civilizations but also re-founded cities on the Greek model, many named after himself. The idea of avenging the Persian invasions of mainland Greece over a century earlier originated with Alexander's father, Philip II (382–336) who trained his citizen army in infantry tactics, replaced the shorter Greek spear with a 6-metre-long pike, and used the gold resources of Mt Pangaeus to fund his war machine. In the decisive battle of Chaironeia in 338 he destroyed the largest military power in Greece, Thebes, and in the following year proclaimed his war of vengeance on the Persian empire. When he was assassinated in 336, his son Alexander III took up the cause and, two years later, crossed the Hellespont with 43,000 foot soldiers and 5500 cavalry. Within four years he had conquered Anatolia, Egypt and Mesopotamia, killed the Persian king Darius and burned Persepolis. As he went he installed his commanders as satraps or regional governors on the Persian administrative model and arranged marriages between Macedonians and local princesses,

163 Bronze statuette of a hunter, *c.* 100 BC. H. 47.5 cm. This bronze possibly represents Alexander the Great or one of his successors in the process of spearing a wild animal, most probably a lion. At Delphi there was a famous bronze statuary group of Alexander and his general Krateros fighting a lion, of which this small-scale figure may be an echo.

164 Silver tetradrachm of Agathocles, king of Bactria, *c.* 190–180 BC. W. 16.22 g. This coin shows Agathocles' predecessor Demetrias I wearing the elephant headdress of Alexander. On the other side is a statue of Herakles holding the lion-skin and club.

which overlaid a veneer of Greek culture in these remote lands. His progress eastward was finally halted, not by the formidable elephants of King Porus of India, but by his own men who rebelled and refused to go further into the unknown. Alexander's short but extraordinary life came to end in Babylon in 323 where he was said to have died of a fever.

Traditionally the Hellenistic period is dated from the death of Alexander to the Battle of Actium in the year 31 BC, after which Egypt under the rule of the last Ptolemy, Kleopatra VII, fell to Rome. Greece itself had come under the sway of Rome much earlier. In 148 Macedonia was made a Roman province, and Greece two years later. Other kingdoms, like that of Pergamon which was bequeathed by its last king to Rome in 133, became part of the Roman empire in a more peaceful way. The Romans were avid collectors of Greek art and often sacked cities as they went; Corinth alone provided hundreds of statues. Many of the official trappings of later Roman art were derived from those of Hellenistic kings.

The first computer

This set of corroded bronze cogs resembling the inside of an old wristwatch was discovered during an underwater excavation off the coast of the Greek island of Antikythera in AD 1900. The sunken ship, dated by coins to around 85 BC, was laden with Greek statues of the Hellenistic period as well as this unique object, now known as the Antikythera Mechanism. Once thought to be modern, it is now recognized as a remarkably complex ancient 'computer', a hand-cranked device with thirty interlocking gear wheels which could chart the movements of the sun, moon and planets. It probably originated on Rhodes where Hipparchos, the greatest Greek astronomer, worked. Not until the fourteenth century AD did mechanical clocks of similar sophistication appear in Europe.

165 The Antikythera Mechanism.

Kingship

Alexander donned numerous symbols of royal power, starting with the lion-skin of Herakles, which alluded to his family's claim of descent from the Greek hero. Because the Macedonians did not initially speak Greek and also practised some very un-Greek customs such as polygamy and drinking their wine undiluted with water, their ethnicity was questioned. Presumably this was decided in their favour by the time King Philip won the horse race in the 106th Olympiad (356 BC). Even Alexander was not fully Macedonian/Greek, since his mother Olympias was a princess from the region of Epiros, north-west of Macedon. Another royal accoutrement was the ram's horns, which may commemorate Alexander's visit to the oracular shrine of Ammon at the Siwah oasis in North Africa, where he was reputedly hailed as a god – that is, the son of Zeus. His conquests in the territory of India resulted in his acquisition of the elephant-scalp headdress. Another guise in which he was often portrayed was that of lion-hunter. Not since the 'orientalizing' seventh century had lion-hunting been depicted in Greek art, and Alexander deliberately adopted this imagery emblematic of Eastern kings, as seen for instance on the famous Assyrian palace lion-hunt reliefs.

Alexander's premature death in Babylon occasioned considerable protracted rivalry among his close followers and generals, some of whom he had made satraps but who later assumed the title of king. Also in the west, Agathokles, the ruler of Syracuse, who successfully waged war on Carthage, took the title of king in 307 BC. Areas far to the east like Bactria (modern Afghanistan) broke away and achieved independence, although they still retained their Greekness, as evidenced by their silver coinage and cities such as Ai-Khanoum which are laid out on an orthogonal plan with a theatre and gymnasium. Eventually three dynasties emerged to form their own independent kingdoms from what remained of Alexander's conquests: the Ptolemies in Egypt, the Seleucids in Syria and Mesopotamia, and the Antigonids in Greece. Because Alexander died childless (he had a posthumous son named Alexander IV with his Bactrian wife Roxane), the succession was always a contested issue, and to legitimize their own claims Alexander's followers issued coinage with his image. His general Ptolemy, who became the first Hellenistic king of Egypt, even went so far as to capture Alexander's funeral cortege, so that the now deified ruler could be buried in his eponymous Egyptian city, Alexandria.

166 Egyptian-style statue of Ptolemy I (305–283 BC) as pharaoh. H. 64 cm. Because this statue is wearing royal headgear (*nemes* headdress with uraeus) and its smiling mouth is characteristic of Thirtieth Dynasty portraiture, it probably represents Alexander's Macedonian general Ptolemy I Soter.

Cities

Although Alexander burned Persepolis in Persia and dismantled communities that rebelled against him, he is credited with establishing some seventy cities as well as restoring monuments. So, for instance, in an effort to reconcile the local population of Babylon and its powerful priesthood he ordered the rebuilding of the great ziggurat of Marduk, which the Persians had destroyed. He contributed to the reconstruction of the monumental Temple of Artemis at Ephesos which had burned down, reputedly on the day of his birth in 356. In the Hellenistic era more people lived in cities that were considerably larger than their Classical predecessors. The population of Alexandria reputedly reached half a million and the city is described by Strabo as having wide streets intersecting at right angles. Only now are some of its famous monuments, such as the Pharos or lighthouse, one of the seven wonders of the ancient world, coming to light through underwater archaeology.

An extremely well-preserved example of a modest Hellenistic town is that of Priene (population *c.* 4000–5000), just south of Ephesos on the west coast of Turkey. It sits on a bluff overlooking the Meander River valley, but in later times its economic prospects declined as the river silted up and blocked access to the sea, leading to its abandonment. The city is laid out in a neat grid plan that is called 'Hippodamian' after the fifth-century urban planner Hippodamos of nearby Miletos, who is credited with codifying principles of urban design. What the plan cannot reveal is that the city is situated on a steep slope, so while the six east–west streets are relatively level, the fifteen north–south ones are sloping, and often stepped. In marked contrast with the irregular Agora of Athens, the city centre at Priene is rectangular, the open-air portion occupying exactly two city blocks and bordered by stoas. The stoa, or colonnaded porch, became one of the major design elements in Hellenistic cities and was used effectively to give a more formal, ordered appearance to open spaces. Like most other Hellenistic cities that were part of an empire, Priene was largely self-governing and so had civic buildings for democratic proceedings, as Athens did. The theatre-like council house is a typical administrative structure. With its three tiers of steeply rising stone seats it could accommodate approximately 640, and would have once had a wooden roof spanning the 14-m chamber. At the southern edge of the walled city were the athletic facilities, a stadium and a gymnasium. The central hall of the latter served as a schoolroom known as an *ephebeum*, where the excavators found students' names scratched on the walls.

Set up on a higher terrace away from the bustle of the city is the temple to its patron deity, Athena. Designed by the architect of the Mausoleum, Pytheos, its plan is highly regularized. The ratio of width to length is 1:2, rather than the Parthenon's 4:9. Just as Polykleitos recorded his canon of human proportions in a manual, so Pytheos detailed his system of architectural proportions in a book about this temple, although unfortunately both texts are lost. A well-preserved inscription attests to the fact that Alexander the Great dedicated this temple to Athena Polias. At a later date a cult statue of Athena, based on that in the Parthenon, was dedicated in the cella. Thus, although the overall plan of Priene is markedly different from that of Athens, many of the structures and monuments deliberately recall that city.

Unlike the small town of Priene, Pergamon was a royal metropolis with a population approaching several hundred thousand. The Attalid kings, so-called for their ancestor Attalos I, established their independence from the Seleucids and founded a magnificent capital city on a precipitous site south of Troy in north-western Turkey. Fanning across the heights of the upper city and oriented in different directions to take advantage of views over the valley or prevailing winds are military barracks, palaces, a sanctuary of Athena, an enormous altar to Zeus in its own enclosure, and a steeply sited three-tiered theatre with a seating capacity of 10,000. Both the temenos of Athena and the civic (as opposed to commercial) agora were framed with stoas. The one to the north of the Doric temple (unusual in this part of the Greek world) housed the great

167 City plan of Priene. Excavated by the Germans in the late nineteenth century, Priene is one of the best preserved ancient cities. The urban design with its uniform house plans demonstrates the democratic ethos of Greece in later Classical times.

168 Inscription bearing the dedication of Alexander of the Temple of Athena Polias in Priene, *c.* 334 BC. H. 1.25 m. 'Alexander the king dedicated this naos to Athena Polias'.

library with its 200,000 books. In fact the Greek word for parchment is *pergamena* because the city became a production and export centre in the second century BC, when papyrus was in short supply. The irregular plan of this city seems chaotic at first glance, but there are deliberate alignments such as the long axis of the Temple of Athena with the Altar of Zeus on the terrace below.

In addition to their own capital city, the Attalids lavished dedications and buildings on Athens, still considered the intellectual centre of the Greek world. Attaloss II provided the Agora with a large two-storied stoa, now reconstructed as a museum, on its eastern side, and Attalos I dedicated an enormous sculptural group on the Acropolis which may have had as many as 120 bronze statues. These statues, as well as another group at Pergamon itself, represented the same mythological battles (Amazonomachy, gigantomachy) as those drawn on by the Athenians for the metopes of the Parthenon. In both instances these battles allude to the Greeks' victories over their barbarian enemies, Persians and Galatians (Gauls) respectively. The great Altar of Zeus at Pergamon, with its long high-relief frieze of a gigantomachy, makes allusions to Athens in a way that any ancient visitor would have understood. The figure of Athena being crowned by Nike, for instance, is a deliberate quote from the east pediment of the Parthenon. What is strikingly different, however, is the style of the Hellenistic relief. With its dramatic poses, variety of textures (scales, feathers etc.), deeply drilled drapery folds, and displays of angst on the part of the wounded giants and their mother (the earth goddess Ge), it is typical of a style known as Hellenistic Baroque, which characterizes the Pergamene school.

Art

After the relatively formulaic art of the Classical period, Hellenistic sculpture exhibits a bewildering variety of subjects and styles. We have already encountered the baroque frieze of the Altar of Zeus, which reverses the norms of Classical architectural sculpture by placing the reliefs *below* the Ionic columns. Alexander's court sculptor, Lysippos, rejected the naturalism of earlier art by claiming to depict men 'as they appeared to be', unlike his Classical predecessors who 'made men as they really are'. Perhaps for this reason Alexander wanted no one else to portray his likeness, as only Lysippos could capture his dynamic personality, 'the melting gaze of his eyes' and the 'lion-like fierceness of his countenance'. As for subject matter, the repertoire expanded from the youthful ideal to include children and the elderly, various states of consciousness such as drunkenness and sleep, the extremely beautiful and the atrociously ugly. Hellenistic sculptors often chose group compositions in order to display a striking contrast between two protagonists: young and old, dead and alive (*Menelaos with the body of Patroklos*), male and female, nude and draped (*Gaul killing himself and his wife*). The ultimate Hellenistic expression of this contrast

171 Opposite: Satyr struggling with a nymph. Roman version of a Hellenistic statue group. H. 76.5 cm. This erotic nude group of an aggressive, animalistic male and a beautiful young girl makes a deliberate contrast. It also exemplifies the Hellenistic use of parody: the nymph's crouching pose recalls a famous statue of Aphrodite at her bath, and the satyr's agonized expression is reminiscent of dying Gauls in Pergamene art.

172 Right: Fat woman riding a pig. Terracotta figurine, made in Egypt, first century BC. H. 13.8 cm. Depictions of old age and the not-so-ideal body were innovations of Hellenistic art.

173 Below right: *Spinario* or boy extracting a thorn from his foot. Marble Roman copy of Greek original of the third century BC. H. 76 cm. Depictions of 'low-life' figures such as this street urchin also became popular in the Hellenistic period.

174 Below: Herakles Epitrapezios, after Lysippos. Limestone Roman version of Hellenistic bronze of the late fourth century BC. H. 52.5 cm. This small-scale image of the larger-than-life Herakles was intended to serve as a table ornament.

175 So-called Alexander Mosaic. From the House of the Faun, Pompeii. At 3 x 5.5 m, this *opus vermiculatum* is a four-colour composition consisting of some four million tesserae or cut stones, each about 3 mm square. It demonstrates a concern for ethnographic accuracy, especially in the appearance and costume of the Persians, who wear trousers and torques.

within a single sculpture is the exotic sleeping Hermaphrodite – a sensuous girl when viewed from one angle, but twisted in such a way that the viewer glimpses his genitals from the opposite angle. All of these and many more famous sculptures are known only from Roman copies.

Scale and proportions also changed radically. Statues might be super-sized, like the Colossus of Rhodes which towered over the city's harbour at a height of 32 metres. This bronze statue cost a staggering 300 talents to construct, and was so huge that humans could not encircle its thumb with their arms. It represented the patron deity of the newly founded city, the sun god Helios, and probably resembled the Statue of Liberty (which stands 46.5 m tall) with its spiked nimbus encircling the head. At the opposite extreme were miniature statues. The sculptor Lysippos is said to have made a small-scale bronze seated Herakles which Alexander carried with him on his campaigns; it was nicknamed the *Herakles Epitrapezios* ('at or on the table').

We know considerably less about painting in this period because little of it survives except a few examples in underground tombs in Macedonia. Although Roman copies were made for wealthy inhabitants of Roman resort towns on the

176 Fragment of a mosaic border with comic mask from Tel Dor, *c.* 100 BC. An example of the superb quality of Hellenistic palatial decoration, this theatrical mosaic in the *opus vermiculatum* technique depicts the mask of a young dandy set within a luxuriant fruit and flower garland.

177 Apulian volute-krater by the Baltimore Painter, *c.* 325 BC. H. 88.9 cm. On the neck of this funerary vase is a head set among scrolling tendrils, while the body shows a marble statue of the deceased in a funerary monument.

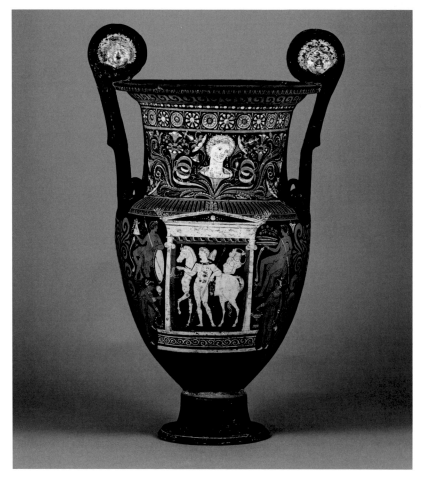

bay of Naples, the fidelity of these paintings to their Greek originals is not easy to gauge, but in the case of the extraordinary mosaic found in the tablinum of the House of the Faun at Pompeii we almost certainly have a faithful copy of a famous lost painting. It depicts Alexander in fierce battle against the Persian king Darius whose forces are being routed. Alexander's calm demeanour as he impales a Persian with his long spear contrasts with the wide-eyed and frightened barbarian king. Scholars still debate whether this is the painting mentioned by Pliny as being 'unsurpassed' (*Battle of Issus* by Philoxenos of Eretria) or a work of the court painter Apelles depicting a later battle (Gaugamela), since he accompanied Alexander on his campaigns.

Apelles was the most famous of all Greek painters and the official court artist of both Philip and Alexander. His images of horses were reputedly so realistic that horses actually neighed at them, and his work in general is noted for its *charis* or Botticelli-like grace. Hellenistic artists also developed an interest in the natural world, and the painter Pausias was one of its leading exponents. His encaustic or coloured wax panel paintings of flowers and vegetal scrolls are dimly reflected in the work of South Italian vase painters.

The intellectual life

Hellenistic society was known for its high level of erudition: cities such as Pergamon and Alexandria vied with each other to create the largest libraries. Scientists, philosophers and writers, often under the patronage of the Hellenistic courts, made great strides in a vast numbers of fields – geography, astronomy, mathematics, acoustics and optics, to name but a few. The polymath historian and scientist Eratosthenes, who was a director of the Alexandrian library, calculated fairly accurately the circumference of the earth with the aid of a type of sundial called a *gnomon*. Also working at Alexandria was the eminent geometrician Euclid, whose work inspired the Syracusan engineer Archimedes. This polymath and inventor created sophisticated siege equipment for Hieron II, tyrant of Syracuse, and he boasted that given a place to stand he could move the earth.

The field of Hellenistic literature is exciting because new texts are still coming to light. Until the beginning of the twentieth century little remained of the late fourth-century comedies of the most famous proponent of New Comedy, the Athenian Menander, although he composed over a hundred plays.

178 Bronze statuette of a seated philosopher. H. 51 cm. This contemplative seated figure wrapped in his himation and with his hand held to his chin as if in deep thought is a typical philosopher type. It contrasts with that of the active, nude and more idealized youthful type adopted for Hellenistic kings.

179 *Apotheosis of Homer*. Marble votive relief signed by the sculptor Archelaos of Priene, late third century BC. H. 1.18 m. Although this commemorative stele came from Italy, it was probably made in Alexandria where there was a shrine to the deified Homer. It exhibits a hierarchical scheme with Zeus seated at the top, Apollo standing with his kithara on the middle level, and Homer being crowned below. Near Zeus stands Mnemosyne (Memory); together they bore the nine Muses, who are the smaller female figures with their attributes. Flanked by kneeling figures labelled *Iliad* and *Odyssey*, Homer is being offered animal sacrifice as though he were a god, but the figures surrounding him are all personifications. Myth and History are at the altar, while beyond Poetry, Tragedy and Comedy raise their arms in homage. Behind Homer stand Time and the World, bearing the likenesses of the Ptolemaic king and queen who founded a cult to the blind bard.

The discovery of his first almost entirely extant comedy *Dyskolos* (*Misanthrope*) was announced in 1957. It is typical of New Comedy in that it lacks topical allusions and political references, and the chorus has been reduced to a musical entr'acte. His plots revolve around misunderstandings, often involving family and children, jealousy and last-minute recognitions, and his characters seem more humane and virtuous – even the slaves and courtesans – than the so-called Old Comedy characters of Aristophanes. A more recent discovery (2001) was the papyrus text of 112 poems of the epigrammist Poseidippos, found in Egyptian mummy wrappings in Milan which are dated *c.* AD 180. This find has considerably expanded the previously known repertoire of epigrams dealing with love and the symposium to a vast array of topics including gemstones, bird omens, dedications and equestrian monuments.

180 Possible portrait of Kleopatra VII (69–30 BC). H. 28 cm. Plutarch recorded that it was her conversation rather than her appearance that was the secret of Kleopatra's success with powerful men such as Julius Caesar and Mark Antony.

The best-known men of letters of the Hellenistic age are the resident Alexandrians Kallimachos, Theokritos and Apollonios of Rhodes. As the librarian at Alexandria during the days of Ptolemy I and II, Kallimachos devised the first library catalogue, arranging the scrolls by subject matter and listing the first line of each. He was an erudite poet and is famous for composing *Aitia,* short poems about the mythical or historic origins of cities, festivals and cults. The Syracusan Theokritos is best known for the idyll or short poem as well as bucolic poetry with its pastoral settings and rustic shepherds. A student of Kallimachos, Apollonios (who was from Alexandria but took exile in Rhodes) composed a long epic poem, the *Argonautika*, rather than short, witty epigrams. It tells the tale of Jason's odyssey to the Black Sea to win the Golden Fleece and his subsequent love affair with Medea. One of the most quoted sections of this poem is the description of Medea's growing love for Jason and her violent emotions. Although in form this epic imitates Homer, in its realism it is purely Hellenistic.

Much of this scholarly poetry borrowed from the past, and a reverence for the earlier titans of Greek culture was manifested throughout the Hellenistic world. Ptolemy IV and his wife Arsinoe III founded a temple to Homer in Alexandria, known as the Homereion. A portrait-type of the blind old bard (see

Chapter 1, fig. 7) is invented for Homer in this period, and possibly also for Hesiod. Like literary epic and hymns to the gods, older styles of figurative art were revived in new, more decorative forms described as 'archaistic' and 'classicizing', and these proved especially popular with the new Roman clientele.

The last word should go to Polybios (*c.* 200–118 BC), the only Hellenistic historian whose work survives in any quantity. His aim was to answer the question of 'how and by a state with what sort of constitution almost the whole of the known world was conquered and fell under the single rule of the Romans in a space of not quite fifty-three years'. He invokes the metaphor of super-natural guidance or *Tyche* (Fortune) but is rigidly logical in seeking the beginnings and causes of Rome's progress to world dominion. Polybios did not live to witness the final demise of Hellenistic hegemony at the Battle of Actium. Shortly thereafter the last remaining Hellenistic ruler, the 'Queen of Kings and King of Kings' Kleopatra VII, who bore the children of both Julius Caesar and his rival Mark Antony, took her own life. Like Alexander three centuries earlier, her legend became even more powerful than the historic facts, but there is no doubt that her death ushered in a new world order.

Recycling the Past

It seems the Greeks will always be with us. Even in the twenty-first century AD, some two millennia after Kleopatra ceded the last vestige of Greek hegemony to Octavian, we are still influenced by many of the achievements of the Hellenes. Athenian dramas are enacted on stages worldwide, the Olympics are held every four years, new buildings continue to rework the Doric and Ionic orders and philosophers still debate the Good and the Beautiful in true Socratic fashion. While the format might change – we can now relive the last stand of the Spartan general Leonidas at Thermopylai in comic book or film – the message remains remarkably the same. Greek values of freedom, heroism, athleticism, individuality and enquiry still lie at the core of modern Western societies. So too do many of the less positive aspects – imperialism, militarism, human bondage and female repression. Ancient Greece was not the perfect world that the nineteenth-century Romantics imagined, but it remains a source of inspiration in manifold ways and in a variety of different and new contexts.

Architecture, sculpture and painting are perhaps the most visible areas of classical influence, although science and medicine are also deeply indebted to the Greeks. For better

181 Rembrandt, *Aristotle Contemplating the Bust of Homer,* AD 1653. The great seventeenth-century Dutch artist painted this imaginary portrait at the request of a Sicilian collector. It depicts the philosopher Aristotle in deep contemplation, with his hand resting on a marble bust representing the epic poet Homer. In his *Poetics* Aristotle discusses the concept of *mimesis* or representation and unity of time, place and action in literature – both of which are important aspects of Homer's *Iliad*. Perhaps here Rembrandt too is meditating on the nature of the arts as handed down from Greek antiquity.

or worse, much of Western art is still judged by the standards and ideals created in the mid fifth century BC. Themes and characters from Greek mythology – Prometheus and Orpheus, for instance, to name just two – continue to resonate with contemporary artists, as Oidipous does in the psychology of Sigmund Freud. In art forms such as theatre, opera, film, dance and literature, both outward style and inner structure as well as content – either directly or via allusion – are regularly borrowed from the classical past. Whereas a dramatic film such as *Troy* (2004) may attempt historically accurate recreations, in this case of the invasion and fall of the Bronze Age city, the Coen Brothers' comic film, *O Brother, Where Art Thou* (2000), was loosely based on the plot and characters of the *Odyssey* but set in Mississippi during the Great Depression. These appropriations of the Greek past have been popular in successive waves beginning with the Romans, continuing in the Renaissance (fifteenth and sixteenth centuries), Enlightenment (eighteenth century), Romantic era (nineteenth century) and into modern and post-modern times. Illustrated here are just a few selective instances of the revival and influence of ancient Greek art and learning.

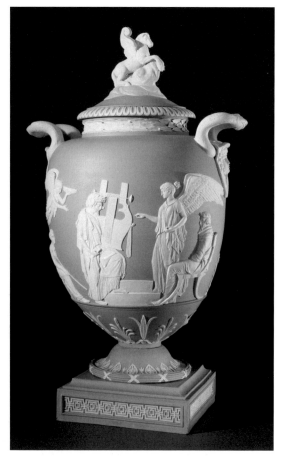

182 Pegasus Vase, after a drawing by John Flaxman on a pale blue jasperware vase by Josiah Wedgwood. Stoneware, AD 1786. H. 45 cm. Wedgwood considered this vase 'the finest and most perfect I have ever made'. In the eighteenth century, when black- and red-figured vases began appearing in abundance from excavations of cemeteries in southern Italy, the potter Josiah Wedgwood was establishing his ceramics factory in Staffordshire. His pre-eminent designer John Flaxman adapted this design from one of Sir William Hamilton's red-figure kraters, although the shape with its Medusa-mask handles was a modern invention. Wedgwood pottery achieved worldwide commercial success, captivating its buyers 'with the Elegance and simplicity of the ancients'.

183 Julia Margaret Cameron, *Teachings from the Elgin Marbles, from Life*. Albumen print, AD 1860. The influential British photographer Julia Margaret Cameron dressed and positioned her two female models in the manner of the goddesses from the east pediment of the Parthenon, which she would have known in the British Museum. By putting wings on her photographic subjects to make them resemble Eros or posing her female friends as sculptures from the Parthenon, she sought to ennoble her subjects as well as the new medium of photography.

184 Above right: Two goddesses from the east pediment of the Parthenon.

185 Opposite: Reclining female bronze sculpture by Henry Moore. Perhaps this twentieth-century British sculptor, who was familiar with the Parthenon sculptures in the British Museum in London, best exemplifies their enduring inspiration in his long series of reclining nudes, produced in both bronze and stone. Although abstract in style, they convey the relaxed pose and massive form of the reclining goddess in the east pediment.

186 Brandenburg Gate, Berlin, designed by Karl Gotthard von Langhaus, AD 1788–91. The
measured drawings of Stuart and Revett in Athens in the mid eighteenth century inspired
works such as this monumental gateway in Berlin, which closely echoes the Propylaia leading
into the Acropolis, notably in the smaller-scale Doric wings flanking the main building.
Architecture from antiquity to the present has employed recognizable elements of the Greek
orders and, perhaps more symbolically, the 'classical' façade of a colonnade topped by a
triangular pediment to convey a reassuring sense of tradition as well as enduring quality.
These elements appear in everything from hallowed churches to secular banks and museums
– and even the front end of the Rolls Royce. The Parthenon itself has been revived for a variety
of buildings, including in 1818 the Second Bank of the United States in Philadelphia, and it
has continued to have an impact on modern architects from Le Corbusier to Alvar Aalto.

187 St Pancras Church, Euston Road, London, designed by William and Henry Inwood, AD 1819–22. This church has not one but two caryatid porches, modelled on that of the Erechtheion on the Acropolis. The Erechtheion was as influential as the Parthenon and reproductions of its monumental doorway and intricate column bases are ubiquitous, but its distinctive caryatid porch has been used more selectively as an appendage to nineteenth-century museums and churches. These maidens with their large jugs are not carved from marble but are modelled in terracotta around cast-iron columns.

188 Leni Riefenstahl, film still from *Olympia*, AD 1936. We end where we began, with Myron's statue of the *Diskobolos* (see Chapter 1, fig. 1). When a talented modern filmmaker wanted to evoke the ideals and beauty of ancient Greece, she chose this statue, which comes to life as the film advances, turning into a real male athlete. It is a telling metaphor of the role of ancient Greece in the contemporary world, one that continues to flourish and inspire.

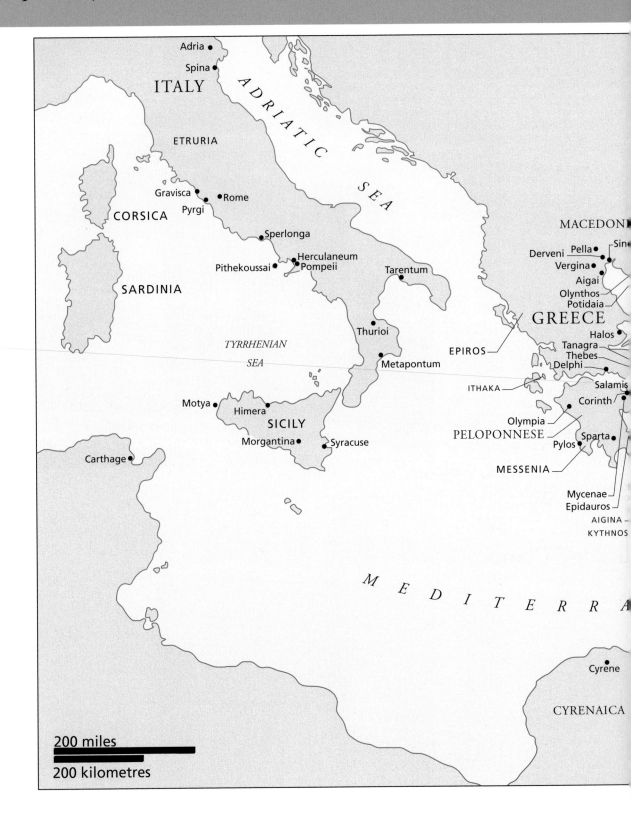

Adria

Spina

ITALY

ADRIATIC

SEA

ETRURIA

Gravisca

Rome

Pyrgi

CORSICA

Sperlonga

Herculaneum

Pithekoussai

Pompeii

Tarentum

SARDINIA

MACEDON

Derveni

Pella

Sin

Vergina

Aigai

Olynthos

Potidaia

GREECE

Halos

Thurioi

Tanagra

Thebes

TYRRHENIAN

Delphi

EPIROS

Metapontum

SEA

Salamis

ITHAKA

Motya

Corinth

Himera

Olympia

SICILY

PELOPONNESE

Sparta

Morgantina

Syracuse

Pylos

MESSENIA

Carthage

Mycenae

Epidauros

AIGINA

KYTHNOS

MEDITERRA

Cyrene

CYRENAICA

200 miles

200 kilometres

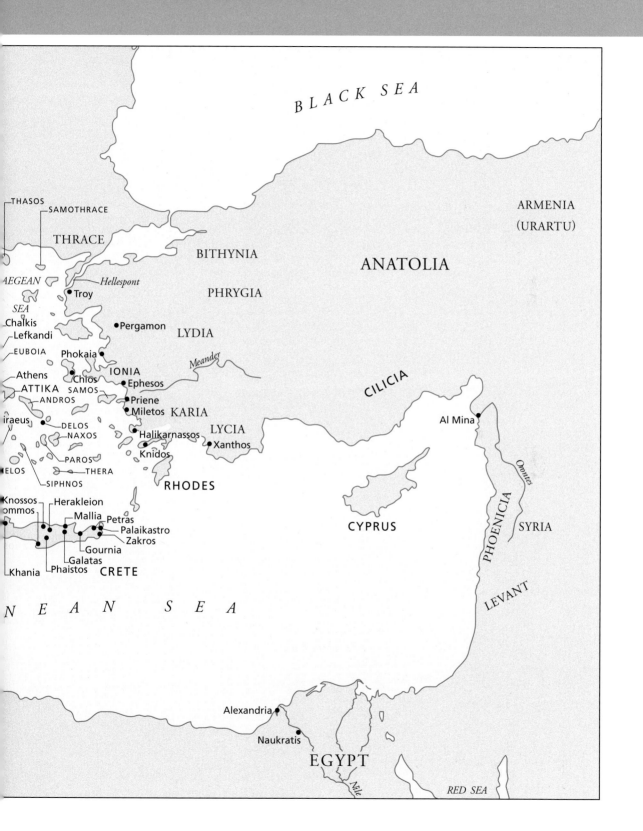

BLACK SEA

ARMENIA
(URARTU)

THRACE

THASOS
SAMOTHRACE

BITHYNIA

ANATOLIA

AEGEAN

Hellespont

●Troy

PHRYGIA

SEA

Chalkis
Lefkandi

●Pergamon

LYDIA

EUBOIA

Phokaia●

Meander

CILICIA

Athens
ATTIKA

Chios●
SAMOS

IONIA
●Ephesos

Al Mina●

ANDROS

Priene●
●Miletos

KARIA

iraeus●

DELOS
NAXOS

Halikarnassos●

LYCIA

PAROS

●Knidos

●Xanthos

ELOS

THERA

SIPHNOS

RHODES

CYPRUS

Orontes

Knossos
ommos

Herakleion

Mallia

Petras

Palaikastro
Zakros

PHOENICIA

SYRIA

Gournia

Galatas

Khania

Phaistos

CRETE

LEVANT

N E A N   S E A

Alexandria●

Naukratis●

EGYPT

Nile

RED SEA

179

Timeline of Key Dates

Chronological Periods

Neolithic	7000–3500 BC
Bronze Age	3500–1100 BC
Early Bronze Age	3500–2000 BC
Middle Bronze Age	2000–1600 BC
Late Bronze Age	1600–1100 BC
Dark Age	1100–900 BC
Geometric	900–700 BC
Orientalizing	700–600 BC
Archaic	600–480 BC
Classical	480–323 BC
Hellenistic	323–31 BC

Key Dates (all dates are BC)

2800–2200	Cycladic culture in Aegean islands
2000	Beginning of Minoan culture on Crete
1640	Eruption of Thera
1600–1450	Shaft graves at Mycenae
1450–1250	Mycenaeans' conquest of Crete; Mycenaean citadels and tholos tombs on mainland
1184	Fall of Troy (traditional date)
1150	Final destruction of Mycenae
1000	Greek migrations to Aegean islands and Ionia
776	Olympic games founded (traditional date)
775	Greek settlement at Pithekoussai, Ischia (Italy)
750–700	Phoenician alphabet adopted
	Homer and Hesiod are active as poets
735	Greek colonization of Sicily and South Italy begins
730–710	Spartans seize territory of Messenia
650–600	*Archilochos, Sappho and Alkaios of Lesbos active as poets*
594	Solon archon at Athens
582	Pythian Games founded at Delphi
581	Isthmian Games founded
573	Nemean Games founded
566	Panathenaic Festival founded at Athens
546–527	Peisistratos tyrant at Athens
546	Persians conquer Ionian Greeks
530–500	*Pythagoras, Herakleitos and Parmenides active as philosophers, Simonides and Anacreon active as poets*
508–507	Reforms of Kleisthenes at Athens
500–450	*Pindar active as poet, Aischylos and Sophokles active as tragedians*
499–494	Ionian Greeks revolt from Persia
498–491	Hippokrates tyrant at Gela

493	Themistokles archon at Athens
490	Battle of Marathon: Greeks defeat Persians under Darius
480	Battles of Thermopylai and Salamis: Greeks defeat Persians under Xerxes; Sack of Athens
479	Battles of Plataia and Mykale; Persian withdrawal from Greece
478–477	Foundation of Delian League by Athens
464	Earthquake at Sparta; Revolt of the Spartan helots
460–400	*Zeno active as philosopher, Euripides active as tragedian, Aristophanes active as comedian, Herodotos and Thucydides active as historians, Pheidias and Polykleitos active as sculptors*
456	Temple of Zeus at Olympia completed
454	Delian League treasury moved to Athens from Delos
451	Perikles' law to restrict Athenian citizenship
449	Peace treaty signed between Athens and Persia
447–438	Parthenon constructed
445	Thirty Years' peace between Athens and Sparta
431–404	Peloponnesian War between Athens and Sparta
430	Plague breaks out at Athens
429	Death of Perikles
421	Peace of Nikias
415–413	Athenian expedition against Sicily
404	Defeat of Athens by Sparta; Oligarchy of the Thirty
400–350	*Plato active as a philosopher*
399	Trial and execution of Sokrates
378–371	Athens and Thebes at war with Sparta
377	Second Athenian Confederacy formed
371	Battle of Leuktra: Thebes defeats Sparta
359–336	Philip II of Macedon
351	Death of Mausolos, ruler of Karia; Mausoleum begun
350–300	*Aristotle active as philosopher, Demosthenes active as orator, Lysippos, Praxiteles and Skopas active as sculptors*
338	The battle of Chaironeia: Philip II of Macedon defeats Greeks; League of Greek states formed under Philip at Corinth
334–323	Alexander's campaigns against Persia
331	Foundation of Alexandria in Egypt
323	Death of Alexander
320–300	*Menander active as comedian, Stoic and Epicurean schools of philosophy in Athens*
270	*Kallimachos and Theokritos active as poets*
241–197	Attalos I ruler of Pergamon
197	Romans defeat Philip V of Macedon
167	Battle of Pydna: fall of Macedonian kingdom
146	Sack of Corinth and Carthage by Romans; Macedonia becomes a Roman province
133	Attalos III bequeaths Pergamon to the Roman people
31	Battle of Actium: Octavian defeats Antony

Glossary

acropolis literally high city, citadel

aegis protective poncho-like garment rimmed with snakes, often worn by Athena

agora market place; the commercial and administrative centre of the city

Amazon mythological female warrior, an opponent of Achilles, Herakles and Theseus

amphora (pl. amphorae) earthenware jar with two handles for the storage or transport of oil and wine

andron principal room of the Greek house, used as a men's dining room

apobates man dressed in heavy armour who jumps on and off a chariot in athletic competitions

apoikia literally home away from home, a Greek colony

apotheosis moment of transformation of a person or hero from human or semi-divine to divine in nature

aristos best man

aryballos small globular perfume flask

aulos reed instrument consisting of two pipes

barbaroi people who were not Greek in language and culture

caryatid female statue used in place of a column

cella inner room of a temple, where the principal statue stood

centaur hybrid creature part horse and part man

chiton belted and sleeved linen tunic worn by women

choregos private citizen who assumed costs of training and outfitting the theatre chorus

chous (pl. choes) wine jug

Corinthian architectural order characterized by a leafy capital

deme parish, ward village of Athens and Attika

demos people, citizen body, common people

diskobolos discus-thrower

dithyramb choral hymn

Doric dialect of Greek, and an architectural order

doryphoros spear bearer

drachm monetary unit, literally a 'fistful' of six obols, approximately a day's wage

dromos road or entryway

echinos lower member of a Doric capital

emporion trading colony

epinetron thigh cover for women working wool

Eros winged god of love

ethos character, enduring aspects of personality

euandria contest in manly excellence

fibula dress pin, brooch

frieze horizontal band of low-relief sculpture

gorgon one of three hideous female monsters endowed with wings and large fangs

griffin hybrid monster combining a lion with a bird's head

gymnasium educational centre for both athletics and intellectual pursuit

gyne married woman

harpy hybrid monster combining a bird with a woman's head

helot native Greek serf-like subject of Sparta

herm pillar with a head of Hermes above and male genitalia below

heroon shrine of a hero

hetaira (pl. hetairai) expensive prostitute, courtesan, usually free in status

himation woollen cloak

hippodrome equestrian race track

homoioi peers, all citizens who had equal rights to hold state office, especially at Sparta

hoplite heavily armed infantryman

horos (pl. horoi) official boundary stone

hydria earthenware or bronze vessel with three handles for water

Ionic Greek dialect; architectural order characterized by a volute capital

HYDRIA

kandilla marble vessel produced in the Bronze Age Cyclades

kanoun basket used in religious processions

kithara stringed musical instrument, lyre

kleos fame, glory

kleroterion jury allotment machine

klismos wooden chair with a high back

koine common language or culture

kouros youth; standing male nude statue

krater mixing bowl for wine and water

kylix drinking cup, usually for wine

larnax chest often used as a coffin

lekythos narrow-necked container for perfumed oil

Linear A earlier of the two Bronze Age Greek scripts, not yet deciphered

Linear B syllabic script of the Mycenaeans in the late Bronze Age

liturgy financial obligation to the state required of the rich

loutrophoros nuptial water vessel

maenad female follower of Dionysos

mechane literally 'machine', crane used in the theatre

megaron literally house, a building characterized by a columned porch and central hall

metic resident alien

metope square panel, often carved, separating the triglyphs in a Doric frieze

naos main room of a Greek temple

Nereid semi-divine sea nymph

Nike winged goddess of victory

nomos custom or law

obol monetary unit, sixth of a drachm

odeion roofed concert hall

oikos household, including both house and family members

oinochoe wine jug

orchestra literally dancing place, a place of action for theatre chorus

ostracism enforced ten-year exile from Athens, decided by counting names of candidates inscribed on clay sherds (ostraka)

paidagogos male tutor or guardian

palaistra exercise or wrestling ground

pankration contest combining boxing and wrestling

parthenos virgin girl, epithet of Athena

pediment triangular space formed by the gable at either end of a Greek temple

pentathalon contest of five athletic events (running, discus, javelin, jump and wrestling)

peplos long woollen tunic; usual Doric garment for women

petasos broad-rimmed sun hat

phalanx tactical formation of a hoplite army, consisting of ranks of heavy infantry, usually eight deep

phiale libation bowl

phratry literally 'brotherhood', social and religious association of citizens

pithos (pl. pithoi) large earthenware storage jar

polis city-state, a political community composed of a principal city or town and its surrounding countryside

polos tall headdress worn by goddesses

prothesis literally 'placing out', used of the public laying out of a body before a funeral

psykter mushroom-shaped earthenware wine cooler

LEKYTHOS

PSYKTER

183

rhyton drinking vessel in the shape of an animal's head

sarcophagus coffin, of stone, terracotta or wood

satrap local ruler of a province of the Persian empire

satyr mythological creature with equine ears and tail, follower of Dionysos

shaft grave burial place in a deep narrow pit, used in Bronze Age by Mycenaeans

skene literally 'tent', scene building in a theatre, dressing room for actors and storage room for props

skyphos deep wine cup

STAMNOS

sophists teachers of persuasive oratory and paradoxical philosophy

stadium track for a foot or chariot race

stamnos storage jar with two handles

stater silver coin worth two drachms

stele gravestone or other free-standing commemorative slab

stoa building whose roof is partially supported by one or more rows of columns parallel to a rear wall

symposium male drinking party

talent measure of weight or monetary value

techne craft, skill or expertise

temenos enclosure of a sanctuary

thetes general term for hired labourers

tholos type of monumental above-ground stone tomb (shaped like a beehive) favoured by elites of the Late Bronze Age

triglyph vertically grooved member of the Doric frieze

trireme three-banked oared warship

tyrant illegitimate, absolute ruler

votive offering object dedicated or vowed to a deity

wanax 'lord', 'master', title of a monarchial ruler of a Mycenaean kingdom

Major Greek Collections

GREAT BRITAIN

Cambridge
Fitzwilliam Museum
www.fitzmuseum.cam.ac.uk
London
British Museum
www.britishmuseum.org
Oxford
Ashmolean Museum
www.ashmolean.org

AUSTRALIA

Sydney
Nicholson Museum of Antiquities
*www.usyd.edu.au/museums/collection
s/nicholson.shtml*

AUSTRIA

Vienna
Kunsthistorisches Museum
www.khm.at/homeE/homeE.html

BELGIUM

Brussels
Musées Royaux d'Art et d'Histoire
www.kmkg-mrah.be

CANADA

Toronto
Royal Ontario Museum
www.rom.on.ca

DENMARK

Copenhagen
Nationalmusset
www.natmus.dk
Ny Carlsberg Glyptotek
www.glyptoteket.dk

FRANCE

Marseilles
Musée d'Archéologie
méditerranéenne
Paris
Musée du Louvre
www.louvre.fr

GERMANY

Berlin
Staatliche Museen zu Berlin,
Altes Museum-Pergamonmuseum
www.smb.museum
Hamburg
Museum für Kunst und Gewerbe
www.mkg-hamburg.de
Munich
Antikensammlungen and Glyptothek
www.antike-am-koenigsplatz.mwn.de

Würzburg
Martin von Wagner Museum der
Universität Würzburg
www.museum.uni-wuerzburg.de

GREECE

Athens
Agora
www.agathe.gr
Benaki Museum
www.benaki.gr
Museum of Cycladic Art
www.cycladic.gr
Archaeological museums and sites
odysseus.culture.gr/index_en.html

ITALY

Bologna
Museo Civico Archeologico
*www.comune.bologna.it/museoarcheol
ogico*
Ferrara
Museo Archeologico Nazionale
*www.archeobo.arti.beniculturali.it/Fer
rara/
index.htm*
Florence
Museo Archeologico
*www.firenzemusei.it/00_english/arche
ologico/
index.html*
Rome
Vatican City
*mv.vatican.va/3_EN/pages/MV_Muse
i.html*
Villa Giulia
www.comune.santamarinella.rm.it
Sicily (Agrigento, Gela, Palermo,
Syracuse)
*www.regione.sicilia.it/beniculturali/dir
benicult/musei/musei.html*
Taranto
Museo Archeologico

NETHERLANDS

Amsterdam
Allard Pierson Museum
www.allardpiersonmuseum.nl

RUSSIA

Moscow
State Pushkin Museum of Fine Arts
www.museum.ru/gmii/defengl.htm
St Petersburg
Hermitage Museum
www.hermitagemuseum.org

SPAIN

Madrid
Museo Arqueologico Nacional
man.mcu.es

SWEDEN

Stockholm
Medelhavsmuseet
www.medelhavsmuseet.se

SWITZERLAND

Basel
Antikenmuseum Basel und
Sammlung Ludwig
www.antikenmuseumbasel.ch
Geneva
Musées d'Art et d'Histoire
www.ville-ge.ch/mah

UNITED STATES

Baltimore, MD
Walters Art Museum
www.thewalters.org
Boston, MA
Museum of Fine Arts
www.mfa.org
Cambridge, MA
Harvard University Art Museums
www.artmuseums.harvard.edu
Cleveland, OH
Cleveland Museum of Art
www.clevelandart.org
Malibu, CA
J. Paul Getty Museum
www.getty.edu/museum
New York, NY
Metropolitan Museum of Art
www.metmuseum.org
Philadelphia, PA
University of Pennsylvania Museum
of Archaeology and Anthropology
www.museum.upenn.edu
Princeton, NJ
Princeton University Art Museum
www.artmuseum.princeton.edu
Providence, RI
Rhode Island School of Design
Museum
www.risd.edu/museum.cfm
Richmond, VA
Virginia Museum of Fine Arts
www.vmfa.museum
Toledo, OH
Toledo Museum of Art
www.toledomuseum.org

OTHER WEBSITES
Greek art
www.beazley.ox.ac.uk
Greek texts and history
www.perseus.tufts.edu
Greek women
www.stoa.org/diotima

Further Reading

General

Lucilla Burn, *The British Museum Book of Greek and Roman Art*. London, 1991

John Camp and Elizabeth Fisher, *The World of the Ancient Greeks*. London, 2002

T. H. Carpenter, *Art and Myth in Ancient Greece: A Handbook*. London, 1991

Paul Cartledge (ed.), *The Cambridge Illustrated History of Ancient Greece*. Cambridge, 1998

Ian Jenkins, *Greek Architecture and Its Sculpture*. London, 2006

John Griffiths Pedley, *Greek Art and Archaeology*, 4th edn. Upper Saddle River, NJ, 2007

Sarah B. Pomeroy et al., *Ancient Greece: A Political, Social and Cultural History*. Oxford, 1999

Jacqueline de Romilly, *A Short History of Greek Literature*, trans. L. Doherty. Chicago, 1985

Loren J. Samons (ed.), *The Cambridge Companion to the Age of Pericles*. Cambridge, 2007

H. Alan Shapiro (ed.), *The Cambridge Companion to Archaic Greece*. Cambridge, 2007

Brian Sparkes (ed.), *Greek Civilization: An Introduction*. Oxford, 1998

Andrew Stewart, *Classical Greece and the Birth of Western Art*. New York, 2008

Dyfri Williams, *Greek Vases*, 2nd edn. London, 1999

1: Rediscovering Ancient Greece

B. F. Cook, *The Townley Marbles*. London, 1985

J. L. Fitton, *The Discovery of the Greek Bronze Age*. London, 1995

Greek Ministry of Culture and N. P. Goulandris Foundation, *Athens: The City Beneath the City. Antiquities from the Metropolitan Railway Excavations*. Athens, 2000

Francis Haskell and Nicholas Penny, *Taste and the Antique: The Lure of Classical Sculpture 1500–1900*. New Haven and London, 1981

Ian Jenkins, *Archaeologists and Aesthetes in the Sculpture Galleries of the British Museum 1800–1939*. London, 1992

Ian Jenkins and Kim Sloan, *Vases and Volcanoes: Sir William Hamilton and His Collection*. London, 1996

Susan W. Soros (ed.), *James 'Athenian' Stuart 1713–1788: The Rediscovery of Antiquity*. New York, 2006

2: Greece in the Bronze Age

John Chadwick, *The Mycenaean World*. Cambridge, 1976

Oliver Dickinson, *The Aegean Bronze Age*. Cambridge, 1994

J. L. Fitton, *Cycladic Art*, 2nd edn. London, 1999

J. L. Fitton, *Minoans*. London, 2002

Kenneth Lapatin, *Mysteries of the Snake Goddess: Art, Desire and the Forging of History*. Boston and New York, 2002

Louise Schofield, *The Mycenaeans*. London, 2007

Emily Vermeule, *Greece in the Bronze Age*. Chicago, 1972

Peter Warren, *The Aegean Civilizations*, 2nd edn. Oxford, 1989

3: The Emergence of Greece

J. N. Coldstream, *Geometric Greece*, 2nd edn. London, 2003

Oliver Dickinson, *The Aegean from the Bronze Age to the Iron Age*. London, 2006

Robert Fowler (ed.), *The Cambridge Companion to Homer*. Cambridge, 2004

Susan Langdon (ed.), *From Pasture to Polis: Art in the Age of Homer*. Columbia, MO, 1993

Ian Morris and Barry Powell (eds), *A New Companion to Homer*. Leiden, 1997

Carol. G. Thomas and Craig Conant, *Citadel to City-State: The Transformation of Greece, 1200–700 B.C.E.* Bloomington, IN, 1999

4: Life in the Polis

John M. Camp, *The Archaeology of Athens*. New Haven and London, 2001

Paul Cartledge, Edward E. Cohen and Lin Foxhall (eds), *Money, Labour and Land: Approaches to the Economies of Ancient Greece*. London and New York, 2002

B. F. Cook, *Greek Inscriptions*. London, 1987

Yvon Garlan, *Slavery in Ancient Greece*. Ithaca, 1988

Mogens Herman Hansen, *Polis: An Introduction to the Ancient Greek City-State*. Oxford, 2006

Victor D. Hanson (ed.), *Hoplites: The Classical Greek Battle Experience*. London and New York, 1991

Oswyn Murray (ed.), *Sympotica: A Symposium on the Symposium*. Oxford, 1990

5: Life in the Oikos

Elaine Fantham et al., *Women in the Classical World*. New York and Oxford, 1994

Robert Garland, *The Greek Way of Death*. Ithaca, 1985

Robert Garland, *The Greek Way of Life*. Ithaca, 1990

Ian Jenkins, *Greek and Roman Life*. London, 1986

Roger Just, *Women in Athenian Law and Life*. London and New York, 1989

Sian Lewis, *The Athenian Woman: An Iconographic Handbook*. London and New York, 2002

Jenifer Neils and John Oakley, *Coming of Age in Ancient Greece: Images of Childhood from the Classical Past*. Hanover, NH and New Haven, 2003

Lisa Nevett, *House and Society in the Ancient Greek World*. Cambridge, 1999

Sarah B. Pomeroy, *Spartan Women*. Oxford, 2002

6: Religions, Gods and Heroes

Walter Burkert, *Greek Religion*. Oxford, 1985

Ian Jenkins, *The Parthenon Sculptures*. London, 2007

Jon D. Mikalson, *Ancient Greek Religion*. Oxford, 2005

Jenifer Neils, *The Parthenon Frieze*. Cambridge, 2001

Robert Parker, *Polytheism and Society at Athens*. Oxford, 2005

Simon Price, *Religions of the Ancient Greeks*. Cambridge, 1999

Roger D. Woodard (ed.), *The Cambridge Companion to Greek Mythology*. Cambridge, 2007

Louise Bruit Zaidman and Pauline Schmitt-Pantel, trans. P. Cartledge, *Religion in the Ancient Greek City*. Cambridge, 1992

7: Wonders to Behold

Sheramy D. Bundrick, *Music and Image in Classical Athens*. Cambridge, 2005

Richard Green and Eric Handley, *Images of the Greek Theatre*. London, 1995

Graham Ley, *A Short Introduction to the Ancient Greek Theater*. Chicago, 1991

Roger Ling (ed.), *Making Classical Art: Process and Practice*. Stroud, 2000

Steven H. Lonsdale, *Dance and Ritual Play in Greek Religion*. Baltimore, 1993

Stephen G. Miller, *Ancient Greek Athletics*. New Haven, 2004

Jenifer Neils, *Goddess and Polis: The Panathenaic Festival of Ancient Athens*. Princeton, 1992

Judith Swaddling, *The Ancient Olympic Games*, 3rd edn. London, 1996

8: The Greeks Overseas

John Boardman, *The Diffusion of Classical Art in Antiquity*. Princeton, 1994

John Boardman, *The Greeks Overseas: Their Early Colonies and Trade*, 4th edn. London, 1999

Luca Cerchiai, Lorena Jannelli and Fausto Longo, *The Greek Cities of Magna Graecia and Sicily*. Los Angeles, 2002

Margaret C. Miller, *Athens and Persia in the Fifth Century BC*. Cambridge, 1997

9: The Hellenistic World

Glenn R. Bugh (ed.), *The Cambridge Companion to the Hellenistic World*. Cambridge and New York, 2006

Lucilla Burn, *Hellenistic Art*. London, 2004

Kleopatra Ferla (ed.), *Priene*, 2nd edn. Athens, 2005

John Onians, *Art and Thought in the Hellenistic Age*. London, 1979

J. J. Pollitt, *Art in the Hellenistic Age*. Cambridge, 1986

Paul Zanker, *The Mask of Socrates: The Image of the Intellectual in Antiquity*, trans. A. Shapiro. Berkeley, 1995

Illustration References

Photography © The Trustees of the British Museum unless otherwise noted.

p. 2 GR 1816,0610.47 (Sculpture 326); **Fig. 1** GR 1805,0703.43 (Sculpture 250); **2** PD 1995,0506.8; **3** © National Portrait Gallery, London (NPG 680); **4** GR 1772,0320.30* (Vase E224); **5** BM; **6** BM; **7** GR 1805,0703.85 (Sculpture 1825); **8** PD 1900,0411.40; **9** GR 1866,0805.2 (Vase E441); **10** GR 1884,0807.1 (Vase A739); **11** © Photo Scala, Florence; **12** © Department of Art and Archaeology, Princeton University; **13** GR 1870,1008.130, Bronzes 7, 15, Vase A870, GR 1959,1104.10, Terracotta B3, Ring 873, GR 1868,1025.57, 1872,0315.5; **14** GR 1890,0110.5, 1843,0507.76, 1889,1212.1, 1890,0110.8; **15** GR 1863,0213.1 (Sculpture A17); **16** GR 1966,0328.1; **17** BM (Kate Morton); **18** © Alberto Pugliese/TIPS/Imagestate; **19** © AKG-Images (photo Erich Lessing); **20** © Burstein Collection/Corbis; **21** GR 1892,0720.2 (Gem 79); **22** GR 1892,0520.8 (Jewellery 762); **23** GR 1910,0423.1; **24** GR 1900,0727.1 (Jewellery 820); **25** © Computerized reconstruction: Mark Bloomfield; **26** © J.L. Fitton; **27** GR 1896,0201.265 (Vase C501); **28** GR 1996,0325.2, 1996,0325.1, Terracottas B7, B5, B6, B11, B12; **29** GR 1897,0401.1535 (Bronze 113); **30** GR 1978,0701.1 (Vase A1093), GR 1978,0701.7 (Vase A1123), GR 1977,1207.6; **31** British School of Archaeology at Athens (drawing J.J. Coulton); **32** GR 1960,1101.18 & 19, 46 & 47; **33** GR 1848,0801.1 (Vase E468); **34** GR 1843,1103.31; **35** GR 1899,0219.1; **36** GR 1864,1007.671, ME 1856,1223.460; **37** GR 1912,0522.1; **38** GR 1997,0815.1; **39** GR 1905,1024.5; **40** GR 1969,1215.1; **41** GR 1870,0315.16; **42** GR 1873,0820.385; **43** GR 1865,0103.28; **44** © AKG-Images/Peter Connolly; **45** CM 1893,0706.1, 1926,0116.693; **46** CM 1906,1103.2591, 1841,0726.288; **47** CM 1906,1103.2591; **48** GR 1906,1215.1; **49** GR 1837,0609.42 (Vase B226); **50** GR 1805,0703.183 (Sculpture 628); **51** GR 1846,0629.45 (Vase B507); **52** GR 1814,0704.277; **53** © AKG-Images (photo Erich Lessing); **54** BM (Kate Morton); **55** GR 1873,0820.129; **56** GR 1805,0703.91; **57** GR 1772,0320.221 (Vase E525); **58** GR 1925,1118.1; **59** GR 1873,0820.724; **60** GR 1860,0404.1; **61** GR 1816,0610.348; **62** GR 1867,0508.963; **63** GR 1848,0619.7 (Vase E68); **64** GR 1868,0606.7 (Vase E768); **65** GR 1954,1018.1; **66** GR 1973,0820.304 (Vase D13); **67** GR 1843,1103.15 (Vase E49); **68** GR 1842,0728.858 (Vase E769); **69** © The J. Paul Getty Museum (AE265); **70** GR 1814,0704.1205 (Vase B598); **71** GR 1890,0222.1; **72** GR 1876,1112.1 (Vase F265); **73** GR 1910,0615.4; **74** GR 1896,1021.4 (Terracotta C214), GR 1911,0416.1; **75** GR 1873,0111.11 (Vase E536); **76** GR 1837,0609.53 (Vase B334); **77** © The Metropolitan Museum of Art, New York; **78** GR 1843,1103.9 (Vase E38); **79** GR 1825,0713.1 (Sculpture 625); **80** GR 1920,1221.1; **81** GR 1864,1007.189 (Vase E396); **82** GR 1887,0725.31 (Sculpture 2001); **83** GR 1884,0223.1 (Vase D65); **84** © Yann Arthus-Bertrand/Corbis; **85** © AKG-Images/Peter Connolly; **86** GR 1816,0610.128; **87** © Ian Jenkins; **88** Photo Gary Layda – Metropolitan Government of Nashville; **89** GR 1864,0220.18; **90** BM; **91** GR 1816,0610.1 (Sculpture 305), GR 1816,0610.11 (Sculpture 316); **92** BM computer-generated photo; **93** GR 1816,0610.47 (Sculpture 326), GR 1816,0610.90 (Sculpture 327), GR 1816,0610.19 (Sculpture 324); **94** GR 1815,1020.5 (Sculpture 526); **95** GR 1895,1028.1; **96** GR 1839,0214.68 (Vase E455); **97** GR 1856,1226.220; **98** GR 1884,0614.31 (Bronze 252); **99** GR 1814,0704.1284 (Bronze 188); **100** GR 1859,1226.26 (Sculpture 1300); **101** GR 1888,1213.1; **102** GR 1873,0820.375 (Vase E410); **103** GR 1865,0712.86; **104** GR 1971,1101.1; **105** GR 1873,0820.375 (Vase E140); **106** GR 1843,1103.40 (Vase B163); **107** GR 1867,0508.962; **108** GR 1849,0620.5; **109** GR 1850,0302.3 (Vase E84); **110** GR 1867,0508.115 (Sculpture 550); **111** GR 1842,0728.034 (Vase B130); **112** © Bildarchiv Steffens/The Bridgeman Art Library; **113** GR 1856,1226.779 (Bronze 223); **114** GR 1847,0909.7 (Vase E271); **115** GR 1816,0610.502; **116** GR 1843,1103.34 (Vase E270); **117** GR 1977,0501.1 (Vase B36); **118** GR 1873,0820.354 (Vase E185); **119** GR 1917,1210.1; **120** GR 1947,0714.18; **121** GR 1805,0703.87 (Sculpture 1831); **122** GR 1842,0728.752, 1907,0520.79b (Terracotta 745), 1879,0306.5; **123** GR 1849,0620.13; **124** GR 1856,1001.1 (Vase B609); **125** GR 1836,0224.173 (Vase E818); **126** GR 1850,0302.2 (Vase E78); **127** GR 1842,0314.1 (Vase B134); **128** GR 1837,0609.83, 1898,0716.3 (Bronze 3207); **129** GR 1876,0510.1 (Bronze 208); **130** GR 1849,1122.1 (Vase B144); **131** GR 1903,0217.1; **132** GR 1898,0716.6; **133** GR 1891,0627.3; **134** GR 1871,0518.2; **135** GR 1864,0220.1 (Sculpture B475); **136** GR 1857,0807.1 (Sculpture 1754); **137** BM computer-generated photo; **138** GR 1861,1127.13 (Bronze 268); **139** © Free Agents Ltd/Corbis; **140** GR 1886,0601.456; **141** GR 1886,0401.1282 (Vase B102.33); **142** CM RPK,p024F.1; **143** GR 1886,0401.1384 (Sculpture B443), AES 1897,0511.197 (EA 1209); **144** GR 1875,0309.24 (Vase B674); **145** GR 1772,0314.70; **146** GR 1823,0610.1 (Bronze 250); **147** GR 1897,0727.2; **148** GR 1882,0704.1 (Vase E695); **149** G&R Department Archive; **150** GR 1851,0416.9 (Vase E447); **151** GR 1848,1020.81; **152** GR 1873,0820.363 (Vase E301); **153** GR 1847,0806.58 (Vase E509); **154** GR 1847,0508.941 (Vase B591); **155** GR 1862,0530.1 (Vase E424); **156** BM; **157** GR 1857,1220.232 & 233 (Sculptures 1000, 1001); **158** GR 1847,0424.3; **159** GR 1872,0515.1; **160** EA 24; **161** CM 1819,0820.1; **162** GR 1908,0414.1 (Jewellery 1628); **163** GR 1868,0520.65 (Bronze 1453); **164** CM 1923,0101.7-1; **165** © AAA Collection; **166** EA 1914,0216.1; **167** German Archaeological Institute, Istanbul archives (drawing A. Zippelius, 1908); **168** GR 1870,0320.88; **169** © BPK/Antikensammlung, Staatliche Museen zu Berlin; **170** © Pergamon Museum, Berlin, Germany/The Bridgeman Art Library; **171** GR 1805,0703.2 (Sculpture 1658); **172** GR 1926,0930.48; **173** GR 1880,0807.1 (Sculpture 1755); **174** GR 1881,0701.1; **175** © Museo Archeologico Nazionale, Naples, Italy/Alinari/The Bridgeman Art Library; **176** © Center of Nautical and Regional Archaeology at Dor/University of California, Berkeley; **177** GR 1772,0320.14 (Vase F284); **178** GR 1865,0712.1 (Bronze 848); **179** GR 1819,0812.1; **180** GR 1879,0712.15 (Sculpture 1873); **181** © The Metropolitan Museum of Art, New York; **182** PE 1786,0527.1 (Pottery 1712); **183** © Victoria and Albert Museum, London; **184** GR 1816,0610.97; **185** © Rune Hellestad/Corbis; **186** © Günter Rosenbach/Zefa/Corbis; **187** © Michael Nicholson/Corbis; **188** © Leni Riefenstahl.

Index